S0-AAZ-772

THE COSTLY CALL

BOOK 2

"Both Caner and Pruitt do a superb job in telling the real stories of God's present-day saints, who take a stand on the name of Christ. . . . Here in the United States believers often forget the cost of being a disciple of Jesus. Many Christians around the world are persecuted by an ongoing barrage of harassment and physical torture even to the point of death itself. Caner and Pruitt not only share the stories of these persecuted saints but also the triumph of the light of the gospel in the darkness of this world. . . . If you are looking for a book that shows how perseverance overcomes persecution and heartache, then read *The Costly Call 2*."

—WILLIAM FRANKLIN GRAHAM IV

"The first four generations of Christians heard about the extreme faith of their relatives, some recorded in the Book of Acts. *The Costly Call 2* is among those published accounts considered a 'modern-day Book of Acts.' Such stories of courageous Christians include Tai of Cambodia who shared that if beatings, ridicule, and rejection are 'what it takes to wake a sleeping world that is hopelessly traveling toward a Christ-less eternity,' Christians around the world are willing to lay down their lives for the sake of leading others into a relationship with Jesus. These testimonies of courage in the face of torture and death will inspire you to live such a faith."

—TOM WHITE
Executive Director
The Voice of the Martyrs

"Read it silently and tears will well up in your eyes. Read it audibly and emotions will make your throat choke up. *The Costly Call 2* is a compilation of the first-person accounts of contemporary believers who live and witness for Christ in hostile surroundings and cultures—believers of whom not only the world but also the church is not worthy. Authors Caner and Pruitt did not set out to write a book about human culture or world religions or reasonable faith or biblical prophecy or even religious persecution as such. But from what they have written you can learn something not learned from many a book intentionally addressed to these subjects. So read it silently to yourself. Or, better yet, read it to the members of your family, growth group, and church. But be sure to read it! Read it and weep! Read it and rejoice! Read it and be informed! Read it and intercede! Read it and give thanks and glory to our God!"

—DAVID J. HESSELGRAVE, PH.D.
Emeritus Professor of Missions
Trinity Evangelical Divinity School
Deerfield, IL

THE COSTLY CALL

BOOK 2

THE UNTOLD STORY

Emir Fethi Caner
H. Edward Pruitt

Kregel
Publications

The Costly Call, Book 2: The Untold Story

© 2006 by Emir Fethi Caner and H. Edward Pruitt

Published by Kregel Publications, a division of Kregel, Inc., P.O. Box 2607, Grand Rapids, MI 49501.

Scripture taken from the New King James Version. Copyright © 1982, Thomas Nelson, Inc. Used by permission. All rights reserved.

For consistency and the benefit of Western readers, most references to monetary amounts are given in equivalent amounts of U.S. dollars.

This book is the account of Christians whose witness goes on, whose sacrifice continues, and whose faith tenaciously abides. For that reason, all names, specific locations, and identifying details have been changed in consideration for the safety of the individuals involved. While each story represents actual events and people, their testimonies are presented in a form that advances the narrative.

Library of Congress Cataloging-in-Publication Data
Caner, Emir Fethi.
   The costly call / by Emir Fethi Caner and H. Edward Pruitt.
     p. cm.
     1. Christian converts from Islam. I. Pruitt, H. Edward.
II. Title.
BV2626.3.C36 2005
248.2'46'0922—dc22   2004027838

ISBN 0-8254-3564-1

Printed in the United States of America

06 07 08 09 10 / 5 4 3 2 1

To the brave men and women within the pages of this work. What a great privilege you have bestowed upon us in allowing us to write your stories.

Contents

The Decay of Religious Liberty

The war on terror is so much larger and more complex than the manifestations we generally hear about. Tentacles of persecution terror reach to lands oppressed by tyrannies and to nations where we expect to find relative openness. We know something about persecution in theory but often we aren't confronted with its pervasive presence in the world.

Even in the United States, the flickering light of religious liberty, a central guarantee of our Constitution, grows more faint. Proponents of tolerance and terror sometimes work toward a common end, to replace genuine freedom with a politically acceptable substitute. Part of the problem is that two terms, *liberty* and *tolerance*, are subtly redefined and confused, with stark, dangerous results. Liberty in relation to religious belief only works if the government protects unalterably the right to believe a set of faith propositions. Yet the common understanding of tolerance is that the government must protect the people from "religious fanatics" and ensure that only mild, secularized religious expressions be allowed to step into politically sacred territory.

Indeed, public policy is coming to be characterized by a minimalist approach to democracy. We can call a system democratic so long as there are free elections. Christians, more than anyone else, must acknowledge that if complete religious freedom is denied, the other basic freedoms of speech, assembly, and press are diminished.

Christians must stand with people in all walks of life and geographical locations and belief systems who face savage acts of terror and persecution. To do otherwise is unconscionable, the moral equivalent to our failure to speak for the Jews of Europe during the 1930s and 1940s. Free people still abandon the powerless in the name of expediency. Satisfied with our own freedoms and saturated in our own prosperity, Western Christians still ignore, disregard, and overlook millions of brothers and sisters who are brutalized by oppressors.

Today persecution is not only in the farthest reaches of the world but on our very doorstep. The West, once known for its adherence to liberty, has succumbed to the intolerance that operates in the name of tolerance. The West has bought into the notion that freedom is not God-given and unalienable. It is regarded as man-given and alterable. And if rulers and voters can grant certain freedoms, they can remove liberties as well.

Across the world political landscape, numerous groups are guilty of persecuting religious people of one kind or another. The most infamous and arguably the most intense persecutors in the world today are fervent Muslims in Muslim-dominated governments. From Saudi Arabia's absolutist Islamic state to Pakistan's institution of blasphemy laws, an escalation in intimidation is in process. One need look only to the blood-soiled fields of the Sudan or the Malaysians terrorized under an oppressive legal code to see why fear grips all of the powerless in Islamic-dominated countries.

Muslims are not the only ones with a worldview agenda that would stamp out religious liberty. In the West, secularists are at the center of a battle to enact laws restricting overt religious expression. In France, for example, one can no longer wear religious symbols in the public school system. Muslim girls can no longer cover their heads in a way they believe is appropriate. Jewish males cannot wear a yarmulke or Christian boys and girls the cross.

Nations such as Australia step into persecution as they attempt to stamp out "hate speech." As this is written, an Australian organization called Catch the Fire Ministries is under court order to apologize for making insensitive, and now illegal, comments about the Muslim community. If the organization's director refuses to show public remorse for his intolerance, he will be imprisoned for speaking ill of another group.

Hindus have been guilty of asserting their will forcefully in areas they control. Muslims, Christians, and others face torture and turmoil within the subcontinent of India. Vigilante mobs trying to purify what they regard as their sacred land and sustain what they believe is sacred law commit murder, rape, and other acts of violence. They are reacting to a secularization that is taking place in historically Hindu societies, even to the easing of the caste system. Hindu-dominated governments have been ineffective in stopping the violence, and Hindus in government often are covertly sympathetic with the mobs.

Similarly, Buddhists also persecute when they attempt to reestablish Buddhist prominence. In places such as Sri Lanka, many in government openly aim to establish Buddhism as the official religion once more. Buddhists receive preferential treatment. Much of the persecution within Buddhist-dominated societies comes from individuals and families. Ancestry and tradition play a central role in the Buddhist community, and those who choose to turn their back on their family history can face serious consequences.

Thus, we as Christians have a monumental task ahead of us. The tide of religious restrictions is growing universally. While some parts of the world, such as the former Soviet Union, are enjoying more liberty, more regions are becoming more closed to faith generally or some kind of faith in particular. Christians must stand up for religious liberty in the global context. We must be grateful when freedoms are expanded and troubled about those places where freedoms are denied.

This is not a day to be pessimistic. We should be glad that Christianity has spread at such a rapid rate and to so many peoples that other worldviews deem it necessary to intervene. We can especially take heart in the courageous faith of the seventeen men and three women in eighteen countries on three continents whose stories make up this book. These true accounts ought to stir us to grieve with those who have counted and paid the cost. We also can rejoice with those individuals who count it worthy to suffer for Jesus' sake. Each of these Christians does rejoice in the Lord, whether they live now in places of persecution or safety. This level of faith asks less for deliverance than for boldness.

We desperately need to learn from these men and women. The essence of Christianity is not found in self-satisfaction, but in selfless sacrifice. We are to esteem others better than ourselves (Phil. 2:3), and thereby emulate the life of our Lord who "humbled Himself and became obedient to the point of death, even the death of the cross" (Phil. 2:8). May He be glorified in our lives, no matter what the cost.

— PART ONE —

MUSLIM PERSECUTION

CHAPTER ONE

PURPOSED TO BE A MASTERPIECE
The Story of DeWei
(Indonesia)

*For we are His workmanship, created in Christ Jesus
for good works, which God prepared beforehand that
we should walk in them.*

—EPHESIANS 2:10

It breaks my heart that my beloved homeland of Indonesia has gone through tumultuous times. Though supposedly a democratic society, Indonesian public policy has come to resemble that of theocratic nations in the Middle East. Once in the early 2000s, nearly a half million Muslims gathered in the streets of Jakarta, the capital city. Their purpose was to publicly declare a jihad against Christians in Indonesia. *Allahu Akbar* ("God is great") and "Death to all Christians" were chanted proudly by the crowd.

They were angered by Christians who were "Christianizing Muslims," an act that the Islamic Teachers Council of Indonesia called illegal, even though the Indonesian constitution protects freedom of religion. Groups of Muslims burned hundreds of churches to the ground. Thousands of Christians were killed in riots, muggings, and home invasions. Christian businesses were burned. Muslim men raped Christian women at will. All the while, the police were either overwhelmed by the volume of violence or they neglected their duties in sympathy with the criminals.

Blaming their troubles on outsiders, like the colonizing Dutch or invading Japanese, these Muslims see Chinese Christians, of which I am one, as the new danger. News agencies and government representatives have tried to explain the violence as ethnic clashes between Javanese and Chinese, but this is not the reason. A new wave of jihad is arising, and my story is just one example of the persecution. My most traumatic moment came when Javanese Muslims raped and killed my beautiful daughter Yi-min.

My grandfather moved from Beijing to Jakarta in the 1920s. He worked three jobs for twenty years and saved as much money as possible. He and my grandmother had four children, my father being the eldest. When my father became a young adult, my grandfather opened his own cleaning business. The business grew from meager beginnings—two employees— to a successful corporation with two hundred workers. In the 1980s my father sold the business for a substantial sum and retired.

When I completed my business degree, my father helped me launch my dream. I opened a hotel designed to attract affluent Chinese businessmen. The hotel was a great success. Within seven years, I repaid my father's investment and expanded the hotel, becoming successful in my own right.

I thought that the world was in the palm of my hand. Everything seemed to be going my way. I was a successful businessman, a father and husband, and I had a new four-bedroom home in an upscale, gated community with two new cars in the driveway. I was a Christian and attended church every Sunday. I gave money to the church and assumed that God would continue to bless me financially. I always treated my employees with respect and paid them well. I was loved and respected by them. Life was truly good.

With such an isolated view of the world, I had only heard of Christian persecution from others. Then one quiet October evening I experienced the pain firsthand. As I left my hotel, three Javanese men attacked me. They beat me with wooden axe handles, saying, "Die Christian, die Christian." Two of my employees stopped them and saved my life. I was in the hospital for eleven days recovering from three broken bones and seven lacerations.

Immediately, I began hearing of churches set on fire while Christians were worshipping inside. Li, my front desk manager, was burned to death while attending a church service. He and sixty-two others had knelt down in front of the pulpit in preparation for meeting their Lord. Li's body was found in the rubble tightly clutching his charred Bible. It was reported that twenty to twenty-five Javanese with guns boarded up the church, doused it with petrol, and set it on fire. After the fire, the police found sixty-seven charred bodies and two young girls shot in the back. Evidently the two girls had jumped from a window before the windows were sealed up. They were found fifty meters from the church.

In the months that followed, I heard of more than one hundred churches that had been burned by Muslims. Times were getting worse. Our church installed a ten-foot-tall chain-link fence around the property. Barbed wire was woven throughout the fence to keep people from climbing over it. We hired four armed guards to protect us while we were worshipping. Every church member was given a pass to show the guard as they entered the church property. There was no entry without the pass.

A few days before Christmas, my wife and I were attacked as we left the mall. As we exited the parking deck two Javanese men threw bricks at our car. Traffic was heavy, so entering the street was difficult. By the time we were out of their reach, three bricks had landed in the front seat and six in the back seat. The windshield, rear window, and passenger window were broken. Once out on the street I saw that one of the bricks had hit my wife in the forehead and imbedded several glass fragments in her head. I slammed on the brakes and took a towel from the back of the car. My wife kept the towel pressed to her forehead while I drove her to the hospital.

The police eventually caught the culprits. They had thrown bricks at nine or ten cars. When the police inquired as to why the men had thrown the bricks, the men replied, "All Christians must die." The days and weeks that followed became increasingly more violent before the worst came.

My daughter, Yi-min, had gone to bed early with an upset stomach. My wife and I had just retired for the evening when I heard someone at the front door. Before I reached the bottom of the spiral staircase, the front door burst open and seventeen Javanese men rushed into my living room. Four men grabbed me and threw me down the steps onto the living room floor. They began beating me and continued saying, "Allah hates Christians. Allah hates you."

Four men dragged my wife down the steps. They were hitting her in the face and chest with their fists. About that time, two men entered the living room carrying a shovel. As I turned to look at them the shovel caught the left side of my head and I lost consciousness for a few minutes. When I regained consciousness, my wife was lying in the corner doubled over, unconscious, and bleeding.

Lying on the floor, I heard a noise. I looked over my left shoulder, and to my horror, one man was molesting my twelve-year-old daughter, Yi-min. One man was raping her while two men held her legs, two held her arms, and one covered her mouth with his hands. As I tried to get up off the cold, marble floor, I found that both of my legs were broken. I could not stand, so I used my hands to drag my body toward Yi-min. I began screaming, "Leave her alone. She is only a child. Leave her alone. She is my little girl." The third or forth time I screamed at the men to stop, I was again knocked unconscious with a shovel.

When I regained consciousness I tried to lift my body from the floor. Just as I lifted myself up to rest on my hands, two men hit me from behind. As though it was precision clockwork, both of my elbows shattered from the blows. I fell to the floor, fracturing my chin as blood was oozing from my mouth. I was forced to watch as man after man savagely assaulted my little Yi-min. With both of my arms and legs broken, I could do nothing but weep. Blood was running down both arms and legs as well as oozing from my mouth. I was powerless to help my little girl. After all seventeen men had raped her, I was forced to watch these men beat Yi-min to death.

My wife was in the corner by the kitchen door with nine broken bones and twenty-six lacerations. I was in the middle of the floor by the staircase with thirty-two broken bones and forty-seven lacerations. I lost five pints of blood before help arrived. And my little Yi-min, there she was near the front door. Her limp little body was lying in a pool of her own blood. How could it get any worse?

As the last man finished his attack on Yi-min and walked out of the front door, he asked me, "So where is your Jesus now? It does not appear he cares for you, Christian." For the first time in my life, I became enraged with God. After all, where was He during all of this? I was not so upset over my own injuries, but just look at Yi-min! How could Jesus allow this to happen to her? She was just an innocent child. Little did I know that I was about to face the spiritual battle of my life.

The police and ambulance arrived two hours after the Muslim men left us for dead. My wife was in the hospital for six weeks, and I was there for nine weeks. I found out that we were not the only family to be assaulted that March night. There were more than one hundred break-ins that night. It was a massive assault. There was no indication that this was a cultural uprising of Javanese against Chinese. It was a religious war of Muslim against Christian. I have personally spoken to more than sixty of the families who were assaulted that night. Only two families were not Christian. Those two families were Buddhists who were new to Jakarta and had the misfortune to move to a predominately Christian neighborhood.

For months, I pressured the police. I gave detailed descriptions of three of the men. To my knowledge, nothing was ever done to find the perpetrators of this heinous crime against my family. The police just did not seem to be concerned. They attributed the assaults to robbery, even though nothing was taken from our home.

My wife and I began going to a counselor at church. We visited him twice a week for nearly a year. It was eight weeks after my release from the hospital before I could set foot in my own home. I stayed in my hotel until I could cope with facing the tragedy we had left behind.

Going home was difficult to say the least. A cleaning crew had sanitized the house, but when I entered the front door, I envisioned Yi-min lying there on the floor before me. I slammed the door, caught my breath, and sat in the car for nearly an hour. Finally, I worked up the courage to go inside. I walked around the living room for some two hours asking God, "Why? Why? Why Yi-min?" Then I left and went back to the hotel. I made several visits back home over the weeks that followed. It took five months before I spent the night in the house. That was the most difficult night of my life. I don't think I slept a wink. I had to do something. So nine months after the break-in, we remodeled our home. It helped a little, but I still see my little girl from time to time.

The counseling began to help. I was studying the Word of God daily. I read the entire New Testament in less than two months. I was growing closer to Jesus every day. Every day I sensed Him telling me to forgive the men who had raped and killed Yi-min. I told Him that I would forgive those men for all they had done to me and my wife; however, they could burn in hell for what they had done to my little girl. At one point, I was willing to forfeit my own salvation if I could witness their torment in hell. I was hurting.

As I continued to read the Bible, I began to realize that I was only hurting my wife and myself. With continued counseling, prayer, and intentional Bible study, I finally was able to ask the Lord to forgive the men who had committed this horror. I even prayed that He would show them the truth of Jesus Christ and save their souls. I was genuine in my prayer. I felt I had come a long way from that March night, but God wanted me to go a little further.

One year after the attack, God completely transformed my heart and changed my life forever. I went to church one Sunday as usual. It seemed like any other Sunday. We showed our pass to enter the fenced compound. We sat in our usual seats. The songs were upbeat and encouraging, and the worship dancers were enthralled in Old Testament dance. The beauty of the songs and the delicate movements of the dancers seemed to lead me to the throne room of God. I felt as though I was ready for a fresh word from God. Little did I know that the Lord would use the visiting preacher from the United States to complete my healing process.

John, a pastor from Colorado Springs, Colorado, was visiting our church. Preaching from Ephesians 2:1–10, he entitled his message, "Purposed to Be a Masterpiece." He focused on verse 10, stating that we Christians are God's masterpiece. He talked about the great artists of the world such as Van Gogh, Rembrandt, and Monet. He explained how the artist decides what colors to paint on the canvas. The canvas has no say as to whether it receives bright, cheery reds, greens, and blues or whether it is filled with browns, grays, and blacks. The master artist makes those decisions.

John explained how God the Master Craftsman has the same right to choose what colors to paint into our lives to make us the masterpiece that He desires. There will be bright colors (the good times in life when things are going well). And there will be times when God will use dark colors in our lives (tragedies, sickness, and persecution). He does this in order that we might be His masterpieces, used to bring honor and glory to His Son, Jesus.

By the end of the sermon, God had broken my heart. I had forgiven the men who had assaulted my family, but I was still somewhat angry with God for allowing it to happen. With tears streaming down my face, I made my way down front to speak with the preacher. I begged Jesus to forgive me for my wicked, rebellious heart. Immediately I was at peace. It felt like a thousand pounds were lifted from my shoulders.

I felt as though I would burst if I did not share what God had just done in my life, so I took the microphone and said,

> As most of you know, my family was brutalized and my daughter killed last year. It has taken me a year to fully come to terms with what happened that night. Today, for the first time, I realize that Jesus Himself does have the right to paint any color into my life that He wishes. I am not asking Him to paint dark colors in my life. However, I am telling Him that if He needs to put more dark colors on this canvas, He is free to do so. I just want Him to be pleased with this canvas. I truly want to be a masterpiece for my Lord.

The months following that worship service were filled with challenges. I went back to work and took control of my hotel again. I hired twelve new employees, ten of whom were Javanese Muslims. I began a Bible study in one of my conference rooms. Within six months, two Chinese and six Javanese had placed their trust in Jesus. Business was going well, and I was thinking of expanding again. I was active in my church and leading a weekly Bible study. The severe pain was apparently behind me. I still missed Yi-min, but I did not weep over her anymore.

I was at home when I received a call from my front desk manager. Someone had set fire to the room where I had been holding the Bible studies. They had caught the man and were holding him at the police station. He was the husband of one of my employees, and was enraged because his wife had become a Christian.

I met with this man three times before his trial. I refused to press charges and told him that I forgave him. He still had to stand trial because the insurance company pressed charges even though I rebuilt the room with my own money. I never accepted any funds for the fire. However, he only went to prison for one year since I refused to testify against him. I even allowed his wife to continue working for me. She continued to grow in her walk with God through the Bible studies.

One night it came to my attention that she was going to be forced from her apartment for nonpayment. With her husband in prison, she was struggling financially. I went to see the landlord, paid her back rent, and paid him for the next year in full. I informed him that he was never to tell anyone that I was the source of the funds. Instead, I asked him to say, "Some Christian paid this for you."

After his release, the man who set fire to my hotel unexpectedly walked into the lobby and asked to see me, which was a violation of his release. The front desk employees were about to call the police when I arrived. He and I went to the restaurant and had a cup of tea. "I want to ask your forgiveness for all the hardship I caused you. I want to repay you. I cannot pay much, but I will pay regularly. Here is my first payment," he said as he handed me about four dollars. I explained that I could not take his money. Then came the shock of my life. "Jesus told me that I must do this."

I dropped my cup of tea and it landed in my lap. I just knew that something was wrong with my hearing or I was dreaming. "Who did what?" I asked. After an hour of explanation, I understood what had happened. This Javanese Muslim man had received a vision while he was in prison. Jesus was telling him how much He loved this man. Jesus instructed him to make things right with me. This man had struggled for nearly a year, believing that he had to set things right with me before he could follow Jesus.

That afternoon in the coffee shop, Jesus allowed me to lead this man in a sinner's prayer. I watched as he became a Christian and disciple of Jesus Christ. I let him know that Jesus had forgiven him, and he owed me nothing. With tears streaming down his face, we became brothers. I immediately hired him, and today he works for me as a night manager. In fact, he makes enough money that his wife no longer works. Now they have two little ones at home, and I am known as Uncle DeWei.

Me, a Chinese man, uncle to a Javanese family—only God can do that. And He did it by painting dark colors on the canvas of my life.

CHAPTER TWO

FOR THE SAKE OF THE FATHER
The Story of Kadir
(Malaysia)

*Do not fear any of those things which you are about to
suffer. Indeed, the devil is about to throw some of you
into prison, that you may be tested, and you will have
tribulation ten days. Be faithful until death,
and I will give you the crown of life.*
—REVELATION 2:10

Malaysia is made up primarily of three people groups: Malays, Indians,
and Chinese. Most Chinese are Buddhists and most Indians are Hindus,
although some are Muslims. As for Malays, all are legally considered
Muslim. Since my father and mother were Muslims, I was an official
Muslim. I am proud to be a Malay, and I have always appreciated my
culture and heritage. In fact, my father traced our family history back to
the first Malay settlers who established themselves in Malaysia, around
1000 B.C.

The rise of traditional Islam in the 1990s created a divorce in our
culture between Muslims and non-Muslims. Islamic law *(shari'a)* is
now implemented in some states, and in these places non-Muslims are

not given the same rights as Muslims. Their testimony is considered less reliable than a Muslim's in court. They cannot inherit a Muslim's property. Economic advantages for Muslims are many. Muslim businesses are given preference under new laws. Non-Muslims are many times not hired to work in Muslim-owned businesses.

With such handicaps, many nominal Christians have converted to Islam in order to succeed in Malaysian society. On the surface it may seem that converting would be advantageous. However, many of these new Muslims suffer tremendously in the long run, not understanding what life is like under Islamic law. As a Muslim, they are subject to amputation if they steal, stoning if they commit adultery, or whipping if they are caught drinking alcohol. If one parent converts to Islam, the children are automatically considered Muslims under the law.

Under shari'a law the most heinous act is to forsake Islam and its tenets. Apostates can be detained for months of reeducation. Women who reject Islam lose custody of their children. Some provinces allow execution of the infidel.

Malaysia, which struggled as a politically fragmented society, has embraced Islam as a unifying force. Under the new order, I grew up attending the mosque on Fridays with my parents and two older sisters. Though I went through the motions of being a good Muslim, I never really cared for Islam as a religion. Perhaps that was due to the fact that I observed so much corruption in the lives of its adherents.

For example, Umar, the imam of our local mosque, lived two houses from me. He instructed everyone in our mosque as to how they should live, but his own life was a disaster. When Umar was angry, he would hit his wife and children. Once I even watched in horror as he kicked his youngest son in the head because his son was vomiting on the front porch. Umar was a brutal man. On one occasion, as I left the mosque, I witnessed him curse at a young woman because her veil had fallen from her head while she was inside the mosque. On another occasion, he made improper advances toward my oldest sister. My father spoke with him, then our family began attending another mosque.

By the time I was twenty years old, I had rejected all religion, especially Islam. I continued my Friday visits to the mosque in order to get a good job. Even before shari'a law, only devout Muslims were hired for positions of importance. I had worked and studied hard to get a good job, and if I had to endure visits to the mosque, it was worth it.

By the age of twenty-four, I was employed as an accountant for the Kuala Lumpur Railway. My office was across the street from the Jalan Hishamuddin, the Moorish-style terminal designed by architect A. B. Hubbock, who also designed the Jam Mosque. My office building was a British colonial adaptation of Moorish architecture, and a reminder that a colonial past was mixed with the present Islamization.

I worked for the railroad company for four years while continuing to go to the mosque. Then one fall, things changed. Amir, a close friend I had known for twelve years, had become a Christian. I watched as his life changed radically. One evening as Amir and I were having dinner at a local café, a Chinese man who had been drinking too much fell across our table and spilled alcohol on Amir. He and Amir fell to the floor. The man came up fighting and accusing Amir of assaulting him. I was ready to fight this drunken man, but Amir calmed him down and sat him at our table. He bought the man several cups of coffee and sobered him up.

As the man, whose name was Wan Kim, began to apologize for causing such a scene, Amir said, "You need not worry, for I forgive you." Then Amir began telling the man about the love of Jesus Christ. An hour later, all three of us went to Amir's home. Amir opened a Bible, the first one I had ever seen, and began reading from the book of Romans. Within an hour, Wan Kim asked Jesus to forgive him, and he became a Christian.

Now I sat in Amir's living room with a former Muslim and a former Buddhist, both of whom had become followers of Jesus. After I left Amir's home, I pondered these strange happenings late into the night. For the first time in my life, I had seen religion make a genuine difference in someone.

Amir and Wan Kim began reading the Bible together every Friday night. I also went to the meetings, though I was still skeptical. Within two months, God opened my eyes to the truth, and I, too, gave my heart to Jesus. I felt as though my heart would burst had I not trusted Jesus. He became so real to me that it seemed He was in the very room with us. I knew that He was God.

Amir, Wan Kim, and I prayed and studied the Bible together. Things went well for nearly a year before we were forced to stand up for our faith. One Friday evening as we were praying together, there was a knock at the door. Six policemen entered the apartment and arrested the three of us. Amir and I were charged with treason against Malaysia, and incarcerated without bail. Wan Kim later was released because he was a converted Buddhist. Since he had never been a Muslim, he was not considered an enemy of the government.

Wan Kim's family had a successful jewelry business in Kunming, China. Wan Kim left Malaysia in order to use his family's funds to assist Amir and me. Wan Kim's father was a powerful financial figure in China and used his influence to secure our release. After some twenty thousand dollars and four months of negotiating, we were released separately, and all charges were dropped.

When I returned home, I learned that my apartment had been rented and my things had been destroyed. I was fired from the railroad and branded a traitor. I was informed that I could have my job back if I would sign a paper declaring my allegiance to Islam. I refused. I thought that I might return to my parents' home for a couple of days until I could make plans for the future. However, my father slammed the door in my face and crassly said to me, "My son is dead. Leave me alone."

Amir was treated in the same manner. His home had been rented to a devout Muslim family, and all of his belongings were destroyed. His father had passed away several years earlier, but his mother wept as he knocked on her door. She pleaded with him, "Please leave me alone or I will face trouble from the police. I am too old to go to jail. Just leave. Just leave." It was clear that the local authorities had threatened her.

We were two former Muslims who had been disowned by our families and disgraced by our country. Our only crime was that we had fallen in love with Jesus. Due to our separate releases from prison, I lost touch with Amir for two years. Then I received a visit from Wan Kim. He was back in Kuala Lumpur. His father had opened up a jewelry store near the twin towers, and Wan Kim was the manager. He wanted to hire me as a salesman. Needless to say, I gladly gave up my position at the auto wash.

The next day, Wan Kim took me to the store. As I entered the front door, I fell on my knees in tears. Standing before me was my old friend

Amir. I had prayed for him for nearly two years but had not seen him since the night we were arrested. It was a glorious day of rejoicing. Amir and I were both quickly promoted to assistant managers and worked alongside Wan Kim for the next two years. Wan Kim, Amir, and I were all visited on several occasions by secret police, and each time we were warned not to be foolish and urged to turn from our Christian ways. In spite of the warnings, we met weekly in the back room of the store for prayer and Bible study.

In fact, Wan Kim had shared the gospel with two other employees, and they also followed Jesus. Amir and I led two others to faith in Jesus. Things went well for a short season, until one of the store employees, who was an agent for the secret police, turned us in.

Two dozen policemen surrounded the store one Friday evening as we were in prayer. They crashed through the front doors in full riot gear and blew open the back door with explosives. Amir and a woman, Saree, were killed in the explosion. Wan Kim and I were beaten with police riot clubs and thrown into jail for conspiracy to commit treason. Unlike the first jail time, policemen now beat me at least once a week.

To my horror, Wan Kim was killed during one of the beatings. The police notified his father that Wan Kim had escaped and was struck and killed by an automobile. When a doctor at the hospital told Wan Kim's father that the wounds were not consistent with wounds found after an automobile accident, the doctor was fired from the hospital.

Wan Kim's father took his body to Kunming, China, to be buried. I thought my life was over since I had no one to defend me from the brutal attacks of the police. In jail, I was beaten with riot clubs, chains, and electric prods, yet this persecution strengthened my faith.

In terribly difficult situations such as this, a believer learns the importance of a powerful prayer life. He also learns how to pray more biblically. I prayed for an hour every morning and at least an hour every evening. In the beginning, I prayed for Jesus to deliver me from the police. But within two months, my prayers changed. Now I asked, "Dear Lord Jesus, help me endure the beatings. Let me bring glory to You, and give me courage to tell others about You."

I found out that His will was that I endure the beatings instead of being delivered from them. During my ten months of incarceration, God allowed me to witness to forty-seven inmates, eight of whom accepted Jesus as their Lord. Three of them were executed within a month of their conversion. Now I know God allowed me to be in prison to tell those poor lost souls who were about to die that Jesus loved them.

One day two policemen opened my jail cell and said, "Kadir, let's go." I thought that they were planning another beating. Instead they took me to the courthouse. As I walked into the courtroom, I saw Wan Kim's father. He had been working behind the scenes for nine months to secure my release, and now that day had arrived. I was presented with a document to sign, and my freedom was a sure thing. However, the document declared that I renounce Jesus and proclaim my faith in Islam. I refused to sign and was about to go back to jail when Wan Kim's father spoke up. He said to the judge, "If you release him to me, I will pay all his fines and take him to Kunming with me to live. He will be my son and I will be responsible for his actions."

I was released after Mr. Kim paid the judge sixty-five thousand dollars. We were taken from the courtroom and placed on the next plane for China. One night, shortly after arriving in Kunming, Mr. Kim asked me, "What is it about Jesus that made you and Wan so committed to Him? Wan died for Jesus and you were willing to go back to jail for Him. Why is Jesus so special?" This hurting man was trying to understand why his son had chosen to die. I looked into those tear-stained eyes and described how Wan and I came to know Jesus as our Lord. I shared with him the power of the Bible studies, and the people who fell in love with Jesus because of Wan. After dinner, I took the entire evening and witnessed to Mr. and Mrs. Kim about Jesus.

Around midnight, Mr. Kim prayed, "Dear Jesus, tonight I, too, accept You just as my son, Wan, did. I trust You with every aspect of my life. I know that You truly are God and I denounce all other gods as false. I will follow Your teachings all the days of my life. Please give me the strength of Wan and Kadir that I, too, might be strong for You."

Mrs. Kim became a believer that night as well.

I went to work in the Kims' jewelry store in Kunming, a position I still have. Not only does Mr. Kim pay me a good salary; he treats me as though I am his real son. He even bought me a car so I could live just outside of town. While my father rejected me, the Lord let me have another father who provided for me. And while persecution took his son from him, the Son of God gave to him another son.

Today I am prepared for whatever the Lord has in store for me, be it suffering or success, pain or prosperity. I have the profound privilege of witnessing to Muslims, Buddhists, and atheists. I am reminded that it is for them that Jesus died.

Ultimately, life is not about what you have lost, but what you have gained. I have gained a personal relationship with the God of the universe and have been allowed to suffer for Him. If I have brought even one minute of glory to Him, then all my suffering and pain has been worth it all.

CHAPTER THREE

Forever Friends
The Story of Bakari
(Egypt)

Two are better than one,
Because they have a good reward for their labor.
For if they fall, one will lift up his companion.
But woe to him who is alone when he falls,
For he has no one to help him up.
—ECCLESIASTES 4:9–10

As a young boy growing up in Cairo, I worked with my parents in the market. My father owned a carpet store in the Khan el-Khalili *souk*, a bazaar that today is much the same as it was when it was built in the fourteenth century. My best friend, Asim, worked with his father selling brass and copperware in the same market. We were the same age, and in our spare time we did everything together. Our favorite pastime was watching the tourists try to bargain with merchants in the bazaar. Every tourist thought he was the world's greatest negotiator. Most of them stopped far short of getting a really good deal. Watching the bartering gave me great enjoyment, but I was most thankful that I was spending time with my best friend.

Asim and I were trained together in the same type of business, and we were also trained together in religious affairs. By age eighteen, Asim and I were personally tutored by Samien Hassan, a direct descendant of the great Sultan Hassan bin Mohammad bin Qala'oun. Samien taught us to quote from memory lengthy passages from the Qur'an and Hadith. On one occasion, I was even allowed to issue the evening call to prayer from the minaret. According to Samien, I was headed for greatness. He told me that I was his youngest student to ever issue the call to prayer.

At the age of twenty-eight, I began teaching in the Madrasa in the Sultan Hassan Mosque. I was the only teacher under the age of fifty. For four years, I diligently taught my students the tenets of Islam and embedded the Qur'an and Hadith deep in their minds. Teaching in the Madrasa was fulfilling intellectually, but spiritually Islam never met my needs. Everything changed when I met Herman.

Herman was a carpet importer from the United States. He and my father had worked together for years. Herman bought only the finest and most unusual of my father's carpets. They had a great relationship, since Herman and my father truly respected each other. Herman was the only Westerner my father did respect.

One summer my father became ill. Since I knew the carpet business and I knew the inventory, my father asked me to stop teaching at the mosque for a few days to negotiate the sale of twenty or so carpets with Herman. Herman and I met at his hotel and went to dinner at Alibabba's, my favorite Middle Eastern restaurant. After dinner, we went to the storeroom where the finest carpets were stored. After four hours of examining carpets, Herman had settled on nine. Since it was after midnight, we decided to meet again the next morning. I escorted Herman back to his hotel because tourist-targeted crime is a problem in a city of 14 million people.

When I arrived at his hotel the next morning, he invited me up to his room for tea since he was still eating breakfast. As I sat down at the table with him, I noticed a Bible lying open on the foot of the bed. I was extremely curious as to why Herman would be reading a Bible. My father had known Herman for years and had never mentioned that he was a religious man.

"I see you have a Bible. Do you find it an interesting read?" I inquired.

"More like life changing," he replied.

"Life changing?"

Herman began telling me of his search for truth. He had read the Bible, the Qur'an, the Dharma, the Talmud, and the writings of Confucius. He had been to Thailand to study Buddhism and to India to study Hinduism. "The only place that I have found truth is in the Bible. I became a follower of the teaching of Jesus ten years ago, and my only regret is that I did not find Him sooner," Herman explained.

My theologically trained Sunni mind was engaged. I began to systematically lay out for Herman why Islam was the only true religion. However, for every truth I declared, Herman countered by showing me the error in my thinking. Before I knew it, we had talked for over four hours. I argued my case for Islam as eloquently as any Muslim I had ever known. Yet Herman's words seemed pregnant with truth. I knew that Herman needed to finish his carpet selections, so I took him back to the store, and the transaction was completed. On the way back to the hotel, I asked Herman, "Would it be possible for us to have dinner before you depart for Cairo? I would like to speak with you further about the Bible."

Herman suggested that we order room service so that we might speak freely and uninterrupted. Dinner arrived around eight o'clock, and I left Herman's room around four AM with a head full of confusion and a Bible inside my briefcase. This was new ground for me. I had read portions of the Bible years before as a textbook, but now I was about to read it in hopes that it would be life changing for me too.

My father was extremely happy with how I handled the negotiations with Herman. "Bakari, my son, you have done well. In fact, you made more profit for me on these twenty-two carpets than I could have made. You should come back to work with me." I gently declined his invitation and went back to teaching in the Madrasa. However, the next two months were hell on earth for me. I was teaching the precepts of Islam, yet I was coming to know in my heart that they were nothing more than lies.

Finally, in late August that year, God confirmed to me that Jesus really is the Way, the Truth, and the Life. My father had a relapse and was rushed to the hospital. When I arrived, the doctors told my mother and me that my father would be dead by morning. There was simply no hope for him. My mind raced. "What could I do? Who would help me?" Then I felt a presence in the room. It was the same presence that I sensed when Herman was with me, but Herman was back in the United States.

"Is that you Jesus?" I asked. That moment a thought went through my mind that was so powerful that it could have only come from God. "Bakari, if you ask me to heal your father, it will be done," the voice said. I leaned over my father and noticed that he had stopped breathing. "Jesus, if that voice in my head was You, then I do believe You. I know that You are God just as the Bible proclaims. Please heal my father. Please do not let him die," I begged as I slumped over his body.

Suddenly, my father started breathing again. He returned to consciousness and asked, "Bakari, my son, why are you weeping?" I explained to him what the doctors had told us, and that he had stopped breathing. In the excitement of the moment, I forgot that I was a teacher of Islam, standing in a Muslim hospital, speaking to my father who was a devout Muslim. I blurted out, "Father, Jesus healed you! You will live. Jesus promised this to me." Before I could shut my mouth, doctors, nurses, and my father were all screaming at me. "Cease this blasphemy! Cease with such lies!"

I was escorted from my father's room by two doctors and taken to an examination room. They determined that I was having a nervous breakdown due to the fact that my father was near death. When I tried to leave the hospital, I was sedated and placed in a private room. I awoke to find that my arms and legs were restrained. Various tests were conducted over the next three days. I was given nine different injections to alleviate depression and bipolar disorder. I was released to my father on the day after he was released. I was so full of prescription drugs that I could not even say my name. I am not sure that I knew who I was when I left that day.

I stayed in my parents' home for the next two weeks. During that time, I stopped taking the medications. At the end of my two-week stay, I was once again fairly coherent. I attempted to speak with my father concerning his miraculous recovery, but the doctors convinced him that they had misdiagnosed his illness. I assured him that he had actually stopped breathing when Jesus healed him. Without even looking at me, my father, whom Jesus had clearly healed, slapped me across the face and called me an infidel.

I returned home to my flat so that I could decide what to do next. I knew that I could not return to the Madrasa and had no desire to return. I knew that I could no longer deceive innocent young men with the lies of Islam. I prayed for three days, asking Jesus to give me wisdom concerning my future. I had lost my family and job. The evening of my third day at home, my landlord entered my flat with two armed policemen. I was immediately evicted, even though my rent was paid six months in advance. I was escorted out of my apartment with only the clothes on my back.

I called my old friend, Asim. He had heard of my decision to follow Jesus and was distant. He advised me that I could come and stay with him for a couple of weeks until I could straighten out my life. However, the day after my arrival, two policemen arrived and arrested me for trespassing. Asim assured them that I was there as his guest, but the police refused to listen and took me to the police station in the worst part of Cairo. With the crime and diseases in Cairo, the "worst station" meant that it was filled with vicious felons, infectious bacterial organisms, and parasitic infections.

I was given two options. I could either return to Islam or I could be incarcerated with the scourge of Cairo. I knew it was wrong to deny Jesus, but I signed a document that stated that I was in the midst of severe depression, and I agreed to enter an Islam reeducation center. I moved back in with Asim for nearly a month. When I failed to attend the first reeducation meeting, I was met on the street and escorted back downtown to the police station. I was released when the police were satisfied that I had merely forgotten about the school.

I realized that I needed to get out of Cairo quickly, so Asim called Wahib, a friend who lived in Marsa Alam, a fishing village on the Red Sea. Wahib said I could stay with him as long as I wished. I was to catch the last bus of the day from Cairo to the village.

Asim escorted me to the bus terminal and gave me three hundred and fifty dollars. I boarded the bus and waved good-bye to my dear friend. I laid my head back on the headrest for what must have only been twenty minutes when police stopped the bus. They boarded the bus with a picture of me that had been taken thirteen years before when I was twenty. When they approached me with the old photo, I assured them that I was not the person in the picture and that I had lost my identification. They removed me from the bus and instructed me to stand beside the patrol car. As the two officers reboarded the bus, I ran as fast as I could.

I realized that I was in the middle of the Cities of the Dead, a part of Cairo consisting of the five major cemeteries of the city. It runs along the base of the Moqattam Hills. Some five million of Cairo's poorest live illegally around these tombs. I was the newest resident. I knew that the police were not likely to chase me through these alleys. There had been clashes between the residents of this unofficial city and the police, and the police did not want to incite another riot.

I walked the streets for nearly two days before I found a place where I thought it was safe to eat. I sat down in the entrance of a broken-down tomb and ate roasted rat and some brown-looking vegetable. I nearly vomited twice. Because I was so hungry, I placed my hands over my mouth to keep the food from coming up. The old street vendor laughed and said, "It may not be tasty, but it is filling." I never dreamed that life could be so horrible. I had never even killed a rat before, and certainly could not have conceived of eating one.

Somehow I survived in the Cities of the Dead for two months before word reached me that a man was searching for me. I knew that it was Asim. When we finally found each other, I was penniless and catching rodents to sell to the street vendor. In return, the vendor allowed me to sleep in his alley and fed me one meal a day. I had never been so happy to see Asim as I was at that moment.

Asim told me I had been declared a traitor of Egypt. There was a bounty for anyone who would assist in my arrest, dead or alive. What was I to do? I could not live like this any longer. Then Asim gave me a glimmer of hope when he opened a bag he had been carrying. As I looked into the bag, I saw a Bible. "Here, my friend. I know that you need this. Maybe it can bring comfort to you," Asim said as he handed it to me. Then he pulled nearly two hundred dollars from his front pocket and handed it to me. He hugged me and promised that he would meet me on the first Monday of each month. Asim kept his promise. He arrived on the first Monday for sixteen months. He brought money on every visit, and occasionally brought new clothes to me.

Soon after Asim's first visit, my new landlord became interested in my Bible. After discussing the teachings of Jesus four times with him, my landlord became a follower of Jesus. Word spread that an Egyptian disciple of Jesus was around, and people came looking for me. Within my first year in my new home, I led sixty people to faith in Jesus. Four men seemed especially hungry for God's Word, so we studied the Bible at least three times a week. We discussed the teachings and tried to apply them to our lives. By the time I had been a resident of the city for sixteen months, there were more than one hundred believers. Some met in their homes or alleys; others gathered for Bible study and worship in the main markets.

Word soon reached the police of a movement of Muslims converting to Christianity. In the late fall, the police sent sixty officers in riot gear into the city. They were offering a reward of one thousand dollars for information that would lead to me. They came into the city every day for five weeks, yet I was never exposed because my fellow Christians hid me in back of an old tomb that was well off the beaten path.

I did not see Asim for nearly three months. The police had been monitoring his actions, and since he did not want to endanger my life, he stayed away. However, when he did visit again in the spring, he had new clothes and a passport to give me a new identity. Asim had borrowed his father's car and told his father that he would be on holiday for three or four days. Asim took me to a friend, who cut my hair. Then we headed toward the Red Sea. We crossed into Israel just south of Elat.

Asim and I stayed at the Grand Hyatt on the boardwalk in Elat for three days. The Grand Hyatt is a far cry from the Cities of the Dead. On the morning of the fourth day, I found an envelope beside my bed. The note inside read:

Bakari, my dear friend. I must head back home. I could not bear saying good-bye, so I left you this letter. Please know that even though I am a Muslim, I will be praying that your Jesus takes good care of you. The seven thousand two hundred dollars in this envelope is a gift for you. You need never repay it. It is all I could gather together for you.

The hotel is paid in full for six more days. Please use the money wisely and take care of yourself. Please do not try to visit me or your family as the police will kill you on sight. Please do not phone me because it will cause trouble for me. Good-bye, my dear friend.

It was signed Asim.

I did just as Asim requested. I used the money to travel from Israel to France, where I now live and work for a Christian businessman's organization.

I miss Asim. He is an extraordinary friend, for whom I am eternally grateful. But I know that unless Asim receives Christ as his Savior, our friendship will one day end. I love him like a brother and want him to find peace in his life. He has been so good to me, so kind to me. Nevertheless, I know that "there is none righteous, no, not one" (Romans 3:10). I am aware that Jesus died for him and loves him dearly. Yet I am unable to communicate that truth to him personally.

The same is true of my parents. They were harsh with me, but I love them, and I believe that deep down they love me as well. It is my heart's desire to see Christ transform their lives as He has mine, though I cannot be the one to share the truth with them.

I have very weighty decisions ahead. I am safe here in Europe, but I want to return home and testify to Asim and my parents that Jesus is the Son of the living God. I want to show the heart of Christ, who Himself proclaimed, "Greater love has no one than this, than to lay down one's life for his friends" (John 15:13). This is the love that Jesus demonstrated to us. This is the love that I should show to those I call my friends as well.

CHAPTER FOUR

Untouchable
The Story of Anwar
(India)

*There is neither Jew nor Greek, there is neither slave
nor free, there is neither male nor female; for you are all
one in Christ Jesus.*
—GALATIANS 3:28

Growing up in Jaipur, India, as a Muslim was difficult for me as a child. I was raised within the walls of the "Pink City," affectionately called that by those who know its soft, red sandstone buildings. My mother sold fabric in the market six days a week, and my father drove an auto rickshaw every day. As a young boy, I was required to attend the mosque at least three times a week, and I could only play with Muslim boys in my own community.

We lived on the edge of the Muslim district. The street after the one on which I lived was in the Hindu neighborhood, and I was never allowed to associate with anyone from there. Though I met many young Hindu boys, and I thought it would be interesting to get to know them, it was strictly forbidden.

As many know, India is a very segregated country. Its society is split into five distinctive castes. Though the castes obviously have to interact with one another, especially in large cities such as Jaipur, one is born into a caste *(varna)* and must marry and die within that caste. Even Muslims adhere to this system, though we recognize each other as part of a brotherhood. It isn't part of our religion as it is among the Hindu.

As the eldest son, I was expected to work from an early age. My younger brother and two younger sisters had to work also, but my family really depended on my income from the time I was twelve years old. By fifteen, I stopped attending the mosque altogether due to my heavy workload. My father had purchased a used auto rickshaw for one thousand dollars. We would drive the rickshaw around town as a taxi. To pay for it, we had to work twenty-four hours a day. My father drove the rickshaw from five o'clock in the morning until nine o' clock in the evening. I drove it through the night.

For nearly a decade, my life was pretty much routine. I worked seven nights a week for my father and occasionally drove during the day as well. On my twenty-second birthday, my father bought a second auto rickshaw and told me I could keep one-half of what I earned from that rickshaw. My younger brother took my former driving duties with my father's rickshaw and I began what I thought was a whole new life. I worked from six o'clock in the morning until midnight seven days a week. Some nights I even slept in my rickshaw so I could pick up a few extra rupees from late-night customers.

Working with tourists, I was able to teach myself to speak English. By the time I was twenty-five, I could speak English well and could even read some things in English. I loved tourists. They had a great deal of money and did not seem too concerned about taxi fare costs. Tourists always paid more for taxis and rickshaws than the locals. They also tipped, so I tried to befriend every tourist I could. I made several friends over the years, and I met one man who changed my life.

Thomas, an American from Atlanta, arrived in Jaipur in early June. He was staying at a hotel near where I keep my rickshaw. One morning as Thomas was leaving the hotel, I pulled my rickshaw beside him and asked, "Sir, do you need a ride?" Thomas wanted to visit the Tiger Fort. I told him that it was merely a forty-five minute drive away, and I would be happy to take him. Thomas said he would hire me for the entire day. On a good day, I earn four hundred to six hundred rupees (ten to fifteen dollars). Thomas offered me one thousand rupees to show him around Jaipur for six or eight hours. I immediately accepted his offer.

That first day, Thomas and I visited the Tiger Fort, the Amber Palace, and the Water Palace. As I dropped Thomas off at his hotel that evening, he asked me to wait for him to change clothes and then take him to dinner at Niro's. Niro's is an upscale Indian and Chinese cuisine restaurant where only tourists and elite Indians patronize.

Upon our arrival to the upscale restaurant, Thomas asked me to join him for dinner. I assured him that I could not do such a thing as I was nothing more than a poor rickshaw driver. The owners of Niro's would not allow a lower caste person such as me to enter the doors, much less eat there. After Thomas pleaded with me for a third time, I hesitantly agreed. As I expected, we were met at the door by the manager, who told Thomas that I was not allowed inside since I was a rickshaw driver. Thomas told the manager that he was a food critic from the United States, and he was in Jaipur to write a story, which was true. The manager allowed me in to eat after he said that.

Thomas and I sampled several dishes from the Chinese and Indian menu. I had never seen such variety. Normally, I ate a small bowl of rice for dinner. About once a week, I mix a piece of chicken into the rice. So this was a real treat. I ate more in that one meal than I normally eat in a week. I ate so much my stomach hurt.

After dinner, Thomas began asking me about my religion. Although I told him I was a Muslim, he wanted to know more. I told him what I believed about Islam. Actually I did not remember much of Islam's teachings since I had not been to the mosque in over ten years. But I dressed and lived as a Muslim. I prayed and thought like a Muslim, even though I had forgotten most of the teachings of my childhood. I was a cultural Muslim, and that was good enough for me.

Thomas invited me back to his hotel, and I accepted. He had bought me an extravagant dinner and he still owed me one thousand rupees. Once we arrived, we sat in the lobby for over an hour. Thomas explained how he had searched for truth for nearly ten years before he found truth in a book called the Bible. I, of course, had heard about the Bible, but

I had never seen one. So Thomas pulled one out of his backpack and handed it to me.

I could not read very much of it because I had not learned most of the English words. Thomas kindly read a couple of stories about Jesus. Jesus was amazing. He could walk on water and turn water into wine. He was truly a prophet of God. At about eleven o'clock, Thomas paid me my fare for the day, and asked me if I would be available for hire the following day. For a thousand rupees I was available every day.

The next morning, Sunday, Thomas wanted to go to church. I chauffeured Thomas to the nearby Protestant church, known as the Church of North India, and he invited me to go inside with him. I agreed to translate for him. I was not prepared for what I saw and heard. People were standing and singing. The music was upbeat and loud. There were even people playing guitars. I was not sure what was happening, but one thing I knew: We never worshipped that way at the mosque. This did not seem reverent enough to be genuine worship of God. Yet, the people seemed happy and at peace.

Moreover, though I was the lowest caste in the church, no one seemed to mind that I was there. In fact, a man of the Brahman caste, the highest caste in India, made up of intellectuals and priests, greeted me and extended his hand in friendship. This was too much to comprehend. I was not even supposed to look into the eyes of a Brahman, much less touch him. And this man was willing to shake hands with me? I extended my hand and for the first time in my life, I touched what I thought was a Hindu Brahman priest. I later found out that he had become a follower of Jesus, and he believed that God created all people equal. That was such good news to me.

Later that day, Thomas and I had dinner at the Pizza Hut, another first for me. Afterward, we returned to his hotel and sat in the lobby for a while. We discussed the events of the day and Thomas explained why the people at the church seemed to be irreverent. "They are just so happy that their sins are forgiven that they love to sing praises to Jesus," he said. "As followers of Jesus they will go to heaven and live with Jesus when they die."

I wanted to believe such a thing, but it was too much to take at face value. Around midnight, Thomas asked me to take him to the airport the following morning. I agreed and went home.

The next morning, I arrived at seven o'clock to get Thomas to the airport for his flight back to New Delhi. As I was saying good-bye to him at the airport, Thomas handed me a gift in a plastic bag. "This is for you, my friend. Read it and find everything in life that you are looking for," he said. It was a Bible, and it was written in Hindi, which I could read. "I will read this," I promised. Thomas departed, and for some reason I was sad. I had never felt that way about any other passengers, but Thomas was different.

Later that evening, I was waiting outside the hotel for anyone that might need a rickshaw, and I decided to look through the Bible. Thomas had written me a letter and placed it at the beginning of the Gospel of John. The note said, "Anwar, my dear friend. Please take time to read this book, as it will change your life. It is more precious than money. This book, the Bible, contains the keys to peace, joy, and eternal life. May Jesus give you understanding as you read." Thomas enclosed three thousand rupees (seventy-five dollars) with the letter.

For the next six hours, I read the Bible. I am still not sure what took place that night, but I felt something happening inside of me. I cried when I read about how they beat Jesus and nailed Him to that cross. It hurt me to read it. Finally, I had to close the book. I could not stand to read any more of it.

The following Sunday morning was strange. I found myself sitting in my rickshaw outside the Protestant church, debating whether I should go in. A man came up and greeted me, saying, "Anwar, are you going to join us today? Please come in and sit with me." The next thing I knew, I was in church reading words in a songbook about Jesus. At first, I read them only in my mind, but somewhere in the middle of the worship time, I found myself singing them out loud. I am not sure I believed the words I sang, but the experience did soothe my soul. The pastor preached a message on forgiveness and that same feeling came back that I had when I read from the Bible the first time. After church, I waited for everyone else to leave so I could speak with the pastor.

I had all kinds of questions about Christians, and why they believe that Jesus is God. The pastor answered all of my questions, and two hours later he asked me a question. "Anwar, you have been shown the truth about Jesus Christ. You now know enough to accept His claims and live by them or reject them and turn away. What will you do this day with the Son of God who died on that cross for you?" With trembling hands and a quivering voice, I replied, "Pastor, I do believe that Jesus is the Son of God. I know that He is the way to heaven. I do not know how I know, but I do know that it is true. I will live for Jesus until I die."

That night, I went home and tried to clarify in my mind how I, a cultural Muslim who had just committed his life to Jesus, could live out the truths of the Bible. I was too terrified to tell my parents. They were cultural Muslims just like me, but they were still Muslims. I knew that if I shared with my friends that I had become a follower of Jesus, they, too, would not have anything more to do with me. This new faith of mine brought serious struggles.

For three months, I wrestled in my soul over such issues until word came to me of my mother's illness. She was diagnosed with cancer and had only a short time to live. I went to her home, told her of my decision to follow Jesus, and begged her to listen to me concerning Him. She was very gracious in listening to me until my father came home. Immediately, he grabbed the Bible from my hand and threw it across the room. "No, wait! I want to hear more about this Jesus," my mother cried. I picked up the Bible and began reading, "I am the way, the truth, and the life," to my mother. I did not notice that my father had left the house. Five minutes later, he entered the room with two policemen.

My father had me arrested for trespassing and treason. I had violated the teachings of Muhammad, and that was unforgivable. My father never seemed to care that I had forsaken the teachings of Muhammad over a decade before; he was simply angry that I had decided to follow Jesus. He was not a devout Muslim, but he hated the name of Jesus. I was released from jail after two days. The police dropped all charges because they did not want to get involved in a family dispute.

Word quickly spread that I was a follower of Jesus, and no Muslim would hire my auto rickshaw. My average income dropped from five hundred rupees a day (twelve dollars) to under one hundred rupees a day. I thought that I would literally starve to death. However, I continued attending the Protestant church. One of the members who owned a small restaurant heard of my struggles and began giving me a free meal each day. Things seemed to be getting better until two Muslim men from the neighborhood mosque threw a large bottle of petrol on my rickshaw and set it on fire.

I barely escaped with my life. The bottle of petrol exploded through the back window of the rickshaw. I was covered in fuel, but jumped to safety when I saw the fire spreading. I described these men to the police but they were never arrested. Speaking to the authorities, the imam from the mosque portrayed me as a radical Christian who hated Muslims and a liar who was seeking vengeance on the two men. Therefore, I was arrested for filing false charges. I spent two weeks in jail and was finally released late Saturday night.

Sunday morning at church, six policemen interrupted the worship service claiming that Muslims had filed charges against the church for proselytizing. The pastor was arrested and the doors of the church were chained shut. I went to the jail to visit the pastor on Tuesday and was immediately arrested for conspiracy to proselytize. When the rest of the church heard the news, twenty-six of them came to visit on Friday. Now, we were all incarcerated. On Sunday morning, when seventeen more church members arrived at the jail for a visit, the police dropped all charges and released us. I guess there is strength in numbers. We all went back to the church, broke the chains with a lead pipe, and worshipped Jesus until late in the evening.

People in the community were so interested in what was taking place, that in addition to our normal sixty or so, we had an additional sixty people from the community. The pastor preached that "the truth shall set you free," and eighteen people became followers of Jesus that very night, two Muslims and sixteen Hindus.

Providentially, one of the new believers was part owner in a luggage store. I went to work for him selling Samsonite luggage to tourists. Just a few months ago, Thomas walked into the store looking for a new computer bag. As soon as I entered from the back room, I saw him standing there holding a bag for his laptop. I rushed up to him to thank him for the Bible and made known my decision to follow Jesus. Both of us had tears streaming down our face. Thomas had looked for me, but the other Muslim rickshaw drivers said I had died in a tragic accident.

God was so good to reunite me with the man responsible for sharing the good news of Jesus with me, which led me to faith in Christ. Though we are a half a world apart, his friendship means so much to me. I want to show to others the love he showed to me when I needed it the most.

I only wish that my mother could have heard the gospel with such clarity and compassion. I can still hear those haunting words from my mother: "No, wait! I want to hear more about this Jesus." I attempted to see my mother after that day. Each time, family members stopped me, and I continued to hear her words in my head, "No, wait! . . ."

The cancer spread through my mother's body and took her life. Wanting to pay my respects, I attempted to attend the funeral. However, my younger brother held me down on the ground while my uncle beat me with a five-foot iron rod. I can deal with the violence toward me, but I have a difficult time coping with my mother's words. As far as I know, she died a cultural Muslim. As far as I know, she is not in heaven. I truly believe that it is my father's fault, but I, nevertheless, try to forgive him.

Even now I can still see my mother's face in pain and hear her voice: "No, wait! I want to hear more about this Jesus." Maybe one day my father will cry out with this expression before it's too late.

CHAPTER FIVE

THE NEW BIRTH
The Story of Parisa
(Iran)

That I may know Him and the power of His resurrection,
and the fellowship of His sufferings, being conformed to
His death, if, by any means, I may attain to the
resurrection from the dead.
—PHILIPPIANS 3:10–11

I was fourteen years old when the Ayatollah Rouhollah Mousavi Khomeini grasped control of Iran from Mohammad Reza Shah. Nearly a thousand supporters of the Shah were massacred. My father's oldest brother, Fariel, was one of them. Within a couple of months, the ayatollah sent a military killing squad to my hometown of Qum to kill the Shah's supporters. In May 1979, I watched as my uncle was one of a hundred men executed for treason. We were told that because the Ayatollah Khomeini lived in Qum, all factions had to be eliminated.

My father, who had served in the military, was spared because he was actively serving in southeastern Iran near the Pakistani border. When he returned home in late September 1979, he knew nothing of Fariel's death. My father was devastated by the news and grieved for nearly a year. Shortly thereafter, Ayatollah Khomeini was taken to Tehran for treatment of a heart problem, and he remained there.

I was glad to see the ayatollah leave Qum. Most of his military personnel went with him, and life returned somewhat to normal. Children could play in the streets again, and people were free to walk through the markets without fear of harassment from soldiers. People did not feel so much pressure to go to the mosque every day. Now we only went on Friday.

In 1982, an Iranian family from Kashan moved to the flat next door. The father was the same age as my father and had served with my father in the military, so they were well acquainted. Our two families became close and would share meals. Nasrin, the oldest daughter in the family, was only a year older than I was, and we became dear friends. Nasrin and I enjoyed shopping in the market for our mothers. It gave us a real sense of purpose. The relationship between our two families grew until one October.

One evening, immediately following dinner, Nasrin and I were washing the meal dishes. I heard my father begin to scream at Nasrin's father. I had never seen my father so outraged. Nasrin's father had brought a Bible out from his bedroom and began to read it to my father. My father called him an infidel and traitor of Islam. My father ordered our family to leave. I was heartbroken. From that night on, my father refused to let me spend any time with Nasrin.

Nasrin and I would sometimes come upon each other in the market as we shopped for our families. We would talk about everything except that awful night. One afternoon as Nasrin and I were leaving the market, my father caught a glimpse of us together. When I got home, he was furious. He accused me of terrible things that I had never even dreamed of doing. When I tried to explain to him that Nasrin and I had accidentally met in the market, he said, "Lies. You tell nothing but lies. Leave my home! You are a disgrace to me. You are no better than those Christians!"

Christians? I did not know that Nasrin was a Christian. She never told me that she was not a Muslim. She dressed like me and looked Muslim, so I assumed that we were just alike. Later I learned that her whole family was Christian. Her father had become a Christian in 1978 through interactions with Western businessmen.

My father refused to listen to me and continued to insist that I leave.

So I walked out of his house. I was a nineteen-year-old Muslim woman living alone in Iran, a rarity to say the least. I had nowhere to go and no one to turn to. Then I thought of Nasrin. After walking the streets of Qum for three hours, I went to Nasrin's home. Her family welcomed me as though I was one of their own.

During the first year I lived with Nasrin, not one person in her family tried to convert me from Islam. However, I watched each of them. I noticed how they responded to adversity and pain. Nearly six months after I left my home, my father came to visit me. He ordered me to return home with him. When I refused—the very first time I ever refused my father—he threatened Nasrin's father. "If my daughter is still living in your home tomorrow night, I will report you to the imam. You Christians will face severe punishment," he said.

Nasrin's father calmly replied, "Anyone is welcome in my home, including Parisa. You do as you must. I will understand." Three days later, Nasrin's father was arrested. They released him the next day. This arrest and release happened five times. I told Nasrin's family that I should leave, but they assured me that I was welcome and that everything would work out for the best. Nasrin's mother reassured me, "Parisa, Jesus has control of our lives. He will care for us." To this day, the family has never blamed me for the persecution they faced.

In April the next year, Nasrin's father startled the entire family with great news: "Nasrin, Jesus has been good to us. He has made it possible for you and Parisa to attend the University of Amsterdam. My brother lives there and both of you will stay with his family as long as you attend the university. Arrangements have been made, so prepare to go. The plane leaves tomorrow." I knew that I had become one of the family, but was I ready to leave my own father and mother behind? I had not spoken to them in six months, but was I really ready for this? Yes, I rationalized, this was my way out. If I left Iran, it would relieve the tension between my family and Nasrin's family.

I packed everything I owned into an old, brown suitcase that Nasrin let me use. It had a hole in the corner and the zipper would not zip up all the way, but that did not matter. The next morning, after my father left the house, I stopped by to see my mother on the way to the airport. I kissed her and told her that I would see her in two or three years. There were lots of tears. I am not sure whether she or I cried the most, but I knew without a doubt that my mother still loved me.

When Nasrin and I arrived in Amsterdam, I was mesmerized by the beauty. The tulips were in full bloom and the outdoor cafés were filled with people eating, talking, and laughing. Couples had blankets spread on the grass in Vondel Park and were enjoying the spring sun. Dogs were chasing Frisbees in the park. Amsterdam was a whole new world, a world of which I could never have dreamed.

By springtime, I was unveiled. What a freedom that was. My new uncle and aunt gave me the freedom to decide for myself, and I chose to remove the years of tradition and bondage. The first time I went out in public without my veil, I felt vulnerable. It seemed I was doing something dreadful. While I was shopping on Leidsestraat, a young man smiled at me, and I felt ashamed—like I had become unclean.

By the end of June, I rarely thought of my veil. I realized that I was not dirty, and I came to understand that there is nothing wrong with a young man smiling at you. Come to think of it, toward the end of May I smiled back at the young man behind the counter at Balvert's Fruitbar.

Nasrin and I had it easy for the first few months. Other than house chores, we just prepared for our upcoming education by reading twelve textbooks that summer. We read one a week, hoping that it would prepare us for class. I quickly learned that immunology was an extremely difficult subject. It was taught in English, and though my English skills were far better than most in Iran, I had a difficult time with certain concepts. It would take four years for me to complete a two-year degree.

During my studies, I began dating a young Dutchman and classmate named Marc. I quickly grew fond of him. He was quite different from the other guys at school. He did not drink alcohol except for an occasional glass of wine. He never cursed or became overly angry. He treated me like a lady. We dated for two years, and he was always a gentleman. He never even kissed me until we had been dating for over a year. I knew that someday I would marry Marc.

Through four years at the university, I watched Nasrin and Marc. They were the only Christians I knew. When everyone else was out drinking, or trying to buy copies of future tests, Marc and Nasrin were different. I saw something in them that made me desire to be more like them.

I began to study the Bible every Thursday night with Nasrin. I also began attending church with Marc in Zwoller, a little town where Marc's father was the pastor of a small house church. I had read the Qur'an many times but it was just words on a page. When I read the Bible, it was alive. In addition, Marc's father was an excellent Bible teacher who explained things very well.

I committed my life to Jesus and trusted Him as my Lord. Though I thought I was free when I removed my veil, on that October day I experienced complete freedom. For the first time in my life, I was truly free. I was free from the Ayatollah Khomeini, free from Islam, and free from the penalty of my sin. If I lived to be one hundred years old, I could never repay Jesus for the liberty He gave me.

The next year was a tremendous time of growth for me, yet a great year of tribulation as well. I graduated from the university, and Marc asked me to marry him. I said yes. We were married in October, just one year after my deliverance from Islam. The day after my wedding, I received news from my uncle that my father and mother had been badly burned in a fire. The burns were severe, and the doctors did not expect my parents to live.

After discussing the issue all night, Marc agreed to let me return to Iran alone. I knew that it would be extremely difficult for him to get a visa. Even if he obtained one, it would cause trouble. Two days later, after being married only three days, I returned to Tehran. On the airplane, I returned to my old clothes. I cannot express the bondage I felt when I veiled again. For the first time in four years, I felt dirty. But this time, I knew I was spiritually dirty.

I was greeted at Tehran airport by military police and taken to my father. He had been promoted to a high-ranking officer shortly after Ayatollah Khomeini's death and now controlled a large number of troops, some of which he would use to hold me hostage. There had been no fire, no burns. It was all a lie to trick me into returning home.

My father had me beaten for leaving Iran. When he discovered my Western clothes, he had me beaten again. After the second beating, I had two broken fingers and a broken nose. He told me that I was a disgrace to him and Islam. He informed me that I had two choices, to return to Islam or to die.

I told him, "Father, please forgive me for the way I left you. I was fearful of you, so I left without telling you. I know that was wrong. But I can never return to Islam. I gave my heart to Jesus, and I will follow His teachings as long as I live." My father became so infuriated that he personally cut off all my hair with a knife.

That night my mother was allowed to visit me for the first time. We both cried all night. The next morning I was scheduled to be executed. My mother announced to my father, "If Parisa dies, then I die. If you take her life, then I will take your life and my own." It was evident that she was serious by the look in her eyes and the tone in her voice. I had never heard my mother speak to my father in such a manner. My father agreed to put me back on a plane to Amsterdam. He promised that within a week I would be back in Europe.

However, two days later, when he found out that I was married, and to a Christian, my own father ordered four women to enter my room and savagely brutalize my feminine parts. The oldest woman said, "You will never enjoy intimacy with your husband, you harlot, and you will never bear children." As she cut me with the knife, the pain was more than I could bear, and I passed out. I awoke the next morning in a clinic. I had been bandaged so that I would not bleed to death.

The following morning I was escorted by my father to the airport and put on a plane to Amsterdam. I was not allowed to see my mother. I guess my father was afraid of what she might do to him if she ever knew what he had done to me. It took me several years to forgive him for his atrocities.

I returned to Amsterdam, and was immediately rushed to the hospital. I lost consciousness in the ambulance because I had lost nearly four units of blood. When I awoke four days later, Marc was standing by my side, holding my hand, and praying. I heard him pleading, "Please, dear Jesus, just let her live. That is all I ask. Just let her live." As my eyes opened, joy filled Marc's face. I had never seen a Dutchman with such a big smile. I remained in the hospital for another week. The day I was released from the hospital the doctor sat down with Marc and me and told us that I would never have a baby. "Parisa, the damage is just too great. I reconstructed everything that I could, but you will never be able to conceive. Most likely, due to the scar tissue, you will never have any feeling either," he said with deep regret.

I walked out of the hospital a broken woman. It took ten years for Marc and I to put our lives together. We went to church like good Christians and played the role well. Yet, deep down Marc and I were angry with God for allowing this brutality to happen to me. After all, we had only been married three days. Everything the doctor predicted came true. There was no baby and no feeling.

In March, Marc's father died of cancer. The last months of his life were truly wondrous. Through his pain, he taught us how to love Jesus even in times of trouble. The night he died, he held Marc in one hand and me in the other. With tears streaming down his face, he said, "Please do not continue to be angry with God. You know He loves you, and He does care for you even today." He died two hours later. I had never seen such a peaceful death.

At the funeral, Marc and I asked Jesus to forgive us for our anger and selfishness. We recommitted our lives to Him. It was a time of genuine outpouring of ourselves. Within days of our recommitment, the little house church where Marc's father was pastor asked Marc to come and lead the weekly Bible studies until they could find a new pastor. Marc agreed and we had a new ministry. Marc taught the Bible every week for two years and then the church asked Marc to be their pastor.

Once again, Marc and I found ourselves in a time of internal struggle. There was no salary for being a pastor. Marc's father was retired, so he did not need extra money. The workload was so great that Marc could not stay in his position as a biomedical engineer and pastor the church. Teaching a Bible study is one thing, but shepherding the flock was totally different. Marc felt, in his spirit, that it was the right thing to do, so he left his job of ten years and became a freelance biomedical specialist. Marc worked from home and had plenty of time for the church. But our income immediately dropped over one thousand dollars a month for the first six months. I thought that we would be forced to sell our car.

Something happened the night that Marc and I prayed, "Jesus, if you want us to sell the car, then we will. We are committed to serving you and will do as you ask." That night in early September, within an hour of our prayer, I had nerve sensations in places where the doctors said that I would never have feeling again. It was amazing. I enjoyed being with my husband for the first time since our wedding. For twelve years, I had suffered discomfort, but now there was joy. I'm not sure what made the difference. I knew that Jesus healed me. I just did not know why. Was it a result of our faithfulness to Him? I really did not know, but I am so thankful to Him for His gift.

The very next month Marc took on new clients and our income increased by over twenty-five hundred dollars. God was pouring out His abundant blessings on us.

In the midst of the blessings, I started feeling ill and finally went to the doctor. I was in the doctor's office most of the day as he ran several tests on me. My heart stopped momentarily when the doctor walked in and proclaimed, "Parisa, you are in perfect health, both you and *your baby.*" I was nearly three months pregnant! I could not believe it. When I returned home, Marc was out. When he walked through the front door about an hour later, I jumped into his arms and said, "Papa, we have to begin thinking about names." With tears streaming down our faces, we kissed and fell to our knees. We must have prayed and praised Jesus for nearly two hours. It was a glorious time.

Later we found out that we were parents of a baby boy, whom we named John Marc. I often dream of his future and how he will be used of the Lord. I am sad that he does not have grandparents to play with, learn from, and to hug. I have not seen my parents in nearly twenty years. Nonetheless, God is faithful. My dream is that we raise our son to proclaim Jesus Christ, even if it costs him dearly. The deepest desire of my heart is that someday he will be a pastor in Tehran. Perhaps that can be possible if Iran opens to the gospel. Perhaps that can occur even if this land remains closed to the outside world.

Whatever the case, it will be John Marc's responsibility to follow the Lord wherever He leads. I can only pray for God's best, and God's will.

CHAPTER SIX

BLESSINGS AND BLASPHEMY
The Story of Mubarak
(Pakistan)

*I tell the truth in Christ, I am not lying, my conscience also
bearing me witness in the Holy Spirit, that I have great
sorrow and continual grief in my heart. For I could wish
that I myself were accursed from Christ for my brethren, my
kinsmen according to the flesh.*
—ROMANS 9:1–3

I do not remember much of my childhood. I loved my grandparents. They were wonderful people who truly loved me. I think I enjoyed my younger days for the most part. However, there were always things in life that never made sense to me. Religion was one of those things. I wondered why I had to go to the mosque every day.

I knew the reason given for those daily trips: "You are a Muslim." That answer was terribly unsatisfying. What was the value in it? The mosque was filled with angry old men who would fuss and fight before entering the mosque, and then fuss and fight once they departed the mosque. Going to the mosque did nothing to affect their lives.

Nearly all Pakistanis are Muslim. Islam is our state religion, and

Islamic law is the basis for our constitution. There are Christians and Hindus in Pakistan, as well as Parsees—descendants of Persian Zoroastrians. Nevertheless, everyone must dress according to the strict Muslim code and follow other Islamic practices. Muslims were allowed to speak of Islam, yet those of other religions were forbidden to speak of their faith in public. My own life was set; my father was a good Muslim, so I was a good Muslim.

When I was five years of age, I watched my father load huge bags of grain onto horse-drawn carts. He worked for a wealthy businessman in Karachi. My father was one of ten men employed to move grain and other dry goods throughout the city. In essence, my father was a dockworker and deliveryman. Our family never had much in the way of material possessions, but I never went hungry as many people did in the 1950s and 1960s.

In the 1970s, Pakistan was shaken by political turmoil. The people were governed by martial law. Then friends of my father's boss rose to power and invited him into the new government. Government business operations were turned over to my father. At this time, I returned home from London, where I had lived for four years, earning a degree in international business.

I encouraged my father to expand the business to neighboring towns and villages. The owner of the business thought that it was a great idea and told me that if I would manage the expansion, he would "make me a wealthy man." He was willing to give one-half of the profits to me if the expansion was successful. Our little shipping business expanded to six towns outside of Karachi, even though the country itself was torn with great internal strife.

However, in 1998, Mohammad Rafiq Tarar became president and things quickly fell apart. After India successfully detonated nuclear devices underground, Pakistan carried out its own series of nuclear tests. The United States imposed economic sanctions against both countries, which almost brought our business to a halt. Conflict with India over Kashmir also erupted again. Pakistan-backed troops withdrew from Indian-held territory after several weeks of fighting. Things were going from bad to worse.

The continual turmoil made it impossible for me to prosper. I sold what was left of my portion of the business. My father, at 72 years old, resigned from his position. I withdrew my life savings of about one hundred thirty-two thousand dollars and moved back to London.

At fifty years old, I was trying to get a fresh start. My degree in international business and experience helped me land a position with a London-based shipping firm. I was placed in charge of all shipping to North Africa and the Middle East. Within four months of my arrival, I met Caroline. She worked in my department and was so kind that I wanted to spend time with her.

The first time I asked, "Caroline, would you like to have tea?" she misunderstood. "No. I just finished a cup on my break," she said.

I tried again. "No, I mean would you like to have tea with me sometime?"

"Sure, anytime," she replied. I was so nervous that I was unable to go any further, so I mumbled, "I will get back with you."

Two days later, I gained the courage to take her to tea. I assumed that we were just having a cup of tea in a hotel coffee shop. Instead we ended up at High Tea at the Savoy. They had sandwiches and desserts as well as pots of tea. It was some affair. I dressed in a suit just to drink tea.

Still, it was worth it. Caroline had such a good time that she suggested that I have dinner at her place.

We dated for nearly six months before I decided that I could not live without her. One Saturday afternoon, I met her at Harrods Department Store. We had tea at the coffee shop, and I said, "Caroline, I asked you here today because I have something I need to discuss with you. I love you and do not want to spend any more of my life without you. Will you marry me?"

I was not prepared for her reply. "Mubarak, I, too, have fallen in love with you, but I cannot marry you. I am a Christian, and you are a Muslim. Our beliefs are just too different. As a Christian, I try to follow the teachings of Jesus. You are a wonderful, wonderful man, but I cannot marry you."

Then with tears in her eyes, she walked away. We were both devastated.

The next week at work we decided to cut off all vestiges of our romantic relationship. I had watched Caroline several months before asking her for a date, and I knew she was different from most other English women I had met. She was so kind, gentle, and pure. Maybe that drew me to her. One week after our break-up, she came into my office with a Bible in her hand.

"I do care for you. Please read these first four books in the New Testament, and then we can have dinner at my house and discuss what you have read," she said.

I read one book every night. Friday morning I informed Caroline that I had finished all four books. She was astonished. She thought that it would take me several weeks. We had dinner Saturday night. That night was like being back in school. She quizzed me on nearly every major event in those books. Finally, she inquired, "Mubarak, tell me what you think is the main point of these books."

My reply made her cry:

> Caroline, by reading these books I have come to understand that Jesus claims to be the Son of God. He performed miracles to demonstrate to people that He truly is the Son of God. All of His friends believed that He was the Son of God. One of His friends, Peter, even confessed openly that Jesus was the Christ. So I searched the Internet to find out what Christ really meant. It meant that Jesus was God Himself. I knew that Jesus and His friends truly believed that He was God. I, too, want to believe. I truly do. But it is foolishness. I cannot believe such fairy tales.

Caroline and I talked well into the night. I genuinely wanted to believe, but it all seemed like nonsense. Before I left her home, Caroline prayed that Jesus would show me the truth.

That night I was awakened by a strange dream of a man clothed in white standing beside my bed. I was paralyzed with fear. I could not even move my eyelids. The man was lamenting over me for not trusting in Jesus. Just before the man disappeared, he proclaimed, "Mubarak, if only you had believed in Me, My son. Then, I would have given you eternal life also. Depart from Me for you may not enter My kingdom."

When I awoke, my bed was wet with sweat. I began to weep. I was fearful that I had made the wrong decision and that Jesus would not accept me. I had heard Him say, "Depart from me." I believed it was all over.

I called Caroline in the morning, a Sunday, and gave the details of my dream to her. She invited me to attend church with her later that morning. I agreed and met her at Piccadilly Circus Station.

I was surprised to see that only about fifty people attended the church. I remembered attending the mosque in Karachi and seeing hundreds of people. I remember thinking that this Jesus did not seem to have a very faithful group of followers. If so, where were they on this particular Sunday? However, when the preacher read about Jesus being crucified for my sins and "all my sin and guilt was placed on Jesus," I was cut to the heart. Afterward, I gushed out, "Caroline, this man Jesus must truly be the Christ! I do not know how I know, but I do know that He is God. What these books say about Jesus is true. Do you think He will forgive even me and give me eternal life too?"

That Sunday morning, Easter Sunday 2001, I surrendered my life to Jesus the Christ. I began going to church with Caroline every Sunday. We studied the Bible together in her home every Friday night. We were married in the church on Saturday afternoon, September 8.

The next Tuesday, September 11, the world was irrevocably changed. Even today I am saddened by the events of that day. I have several American friends who live in New York, and I continue to pray for their safety.

In March, I received word that my father, now in his mid-seventies, was on his deathbed; I made arrangements to visit him. Thoughts of my father spending eternity separated from Jesus brought genuine fear. I could not let him die without telling him about Jesus. Also, my family had never seen Caroline, and I wanted them to meet her. So Caroline and I flew to Karachi. During the flight, I begged Jesus to please let my father live long enough for me to tell him the good news about Jesus.

Upon my arrival, I was informed that my father was not coherent and would not understand anything I said to him. For two days, I sat by his bed praying for him. Finally, on the second night I felt the touch of his hand, and I heard the words, "Mubarak, you are home, my son." We talked for nearly an hour, then I said to him, "Father, I have urgent business with you. Please listen closely because you must believe what I am about to tell you."

Gently gripping my hand, my precious father replied,

Son, I know why you have come. Jesus is waiting for me tonight. He appeared to me in a dream two years ago and told me that you, too, were going to be His follower. Your mother, two sisters, and I are all followers of Jesus. How about you, son? Have you, too, seen His glory? I will be with Him soon. Get ready, for your day too will come. I love you, Mubarak. You are a good son.

Suddenly, without me even saying anything, my father's grip on my hand increased and then went limp. He had died.

For a moment, I thought that it was all an illusion or dream. But then I walked into the living room and whispered into my mother's ear, "Papa just went to be with Jesus." I was not sure what her response would be. I was certain something would happen. With tears beginning to puddle in her eyes, my mother said, "Son, your father is at peace. Someday I, too, will join him." I could not have heard any words more precious to my heart. That night was a great night of joy and peace. But it would be short-lived.

That next morning, I made arrangements for my father to have a Christian burial. Little did I realize the problems that it would create. All of his friends condemned me saying, "You infidel. Your father was a Muslim. He must have a Muslim burial. He deserves it. Now see to it." Since my mother was going to remain in Karachi after my father's death, I consulted her. I did not want to cause harm to come to her. She told me she would abide by my wishes, but she preferred that I not observe Muslim traditions concerning my father. So I buried my father in a Christian ceremony rather than a Muslim one.

During my absence from Pakistan, the owner of the business for whom we had worked had become even more influential. After the funeral, he visited my mother and me and demanded an explanation. I told him of my father's conversion and how I also had come to faith in Jesus. I told him that Jesus is God. "Please understand. Jesus is the true God. He is much greater than Muhammad." The man was furious. He called me an infidel worthy of death. He ordered me to leave Pakistan immediately or face the death penalty for blasphemy as prescribed in Section 295c of Pakistan's constitution.

My mother was very weak and frail and wanted to live with my eldest sister and her husband, so she never admitted that she and the rest of the family also were Christians. I kissed my mother good-bye, then Caroline and I were escorted to the airport. We were put on the next flight to London and were warned, "If you ever show your face in Pakistan again, you will be executed for blasphemy."

Caroline and I returned home and resumed our lives. A time of spiritual growth ensued. The following year, I taught a weekly Bible study for young men, who were mostly in their twenties and thirties. Once again, life returned to normal. I never communicated with my mother because I did not want to endanger her life. However, one day I received a letter informing me that my mother was gravely ill. The letter ended by saying, "Mubarak, do not return home. Mother is ready to die in peace. She has made peace with God. Do not endanger your life. She asked me to tell you that she will see you in heaven someday." I knew that my mother had released me from my obligations, and I was relieved.

Yet, I just could not leave well enough alone. After praying intensely for nine hours, I told Caroline that I had to go to my mother. "Go, Mubarak, Jesus will take care of you. He who is in you is greater than he who is in this world. I will see you again, my husband." After lots of tears and kisses, I left for Karachi.

I knew authorities would be watching for me, so I flew to New Delhi, India, and took a flight to Kashmir. A friend met me in Kashmir, brought me some of his traditional Pakistani clothing, and drove me to Islamabad. In Islamabad, I boarded the train for Karachi. When the train arrived, ten or twelve policemen approached the doors. I was not sure who they were looking for, but I knew if I got off the train, my friend and I could be in real trouble. I was traveling on his papers. If I were caught with his credentials, both of us would face the death penalty.

One of the policemen that boarded the train asked for my papers and wanted to know my destination. I told him I was headed for Kaimari, just south of Karachi, to visit an old friend. He looked sternly at my face for a moment and then moved on throughout the train. After about a thirty-minute delay, the train proceeded on to Kaimari.

I disembarked the train in Kaimari and hired an old man to drive me back to Karachi. When we were three blocks from my sister's home, I decided to walk the rest of the way. I prayed every step of the way. As I turned the corner toward my sister's home I noticed two policemen standing across the street outside a little café that was closed. The hair on the back of my neck stood up and my legs began to tremble. I turned back and ducked behind a neighbor's house and then passed through the backyards of two other neighbors. I gently knocked on my sister's bedroom window. When she opened the window, she began to sob. Little did I know that there would be a policeman *in* her home as well. As it turns out, he was an old friend. He was compelled to arrest me, but he allowed me to leave my friend's traveling papers with my sister. That way only one of us would be put to death.

I stayed in jail for four weeks. No one was allowed to visit me except for the government official that I had known so long. He visited three times. Each time, I testified how much Jesus loved him. His response each time was, "Mubarak, you do realize that you are about to die for blasphemy, do you not? Why must you continue to try to convert me?" I assured him that I would be with Jesus upon my death, and I simply wanted him there also.

One month into my incarceration, I was taken from my cell with a hood over my head. I thought that the time had come, and I was about to be beheaded. I was loaded into the back of a car and driven to a private airstrip outside of town. I was then put on a small twin-engine jet with one pilot and an armed guard. We flew so close to the mountains that I was certain we would crash. We finally landed in Jammu, India, where I was told to get off the plane and then given an envelope.

I made my way to a guesthouse in Jammu and spent the night. In my room, I opened the envelope. It contained a letter from my friend in the government:

> At great risk to my own life, I have set you free. Once you and I were good friends. You were faithful to me as a business partner and we made a great deal of money together. Your mother died the fourth night after I arrested you. Her dying words were telling me that I, too, needed Jesus. She died in peace, and I allowed her a Christian

funeral at the request of your sister. I do not know why your faith in Jesus is so strong, but I admire you for it. Please, my friend, never come back to Pakistan or I may be forced to execute you. Your escape took place while in my custody, and I will deal with that. Please do not force me to do something that I will regret. Go and live your life. Forget Pakistan.

I returned home to London within a few days, intensely grateful to see my wife again.

I realize that I risked my relationship with my wife in order to say good-bye to my mother, but I have no regrets and neither does Caroline. Today, we are expecting our first child. Now, my responsibilities are greater than ever. I yearn to see my baby grow up and live for the Lord. Yet, a part of me still wants to share Jesus with Pakistanis who still walk in darkness. I wrestle continuously between two worlds. I need to be a good husband and a good father. My family needs me. But so do my kinsmen in the flesh.

Ultimately, any risk I take must be bathed in prayer and solidified by the reading of God's Word. I never want to do less than His will, but I never want to do more than He desires either.

— PART TWO —

HINDU PERSECUTION

CHAPTER SEVEN

A Pilgrim's Progress
The Story of Durjaya
(Nepal)

*In this you greatly rejoice, though now for a little while, if
need be, you have been grieved by various trials, that the
genuineness of your faith, being much more precious than
gold that perishes, though it is tested by fire, may be found
to praise, honor, and glory at the revelation of Jesus Christ.*
—1 PETER 1:6–7

My earliest memory is of my grandfather's body being laid on wood stacked beside the riverbank. He was wrapped in a burial cloth, and I watched with horror as my father set fire to the wood. As an eight-year-old boy, I trembled with fear as the fire consumed his body. Then I watched as a portion of his ashes were scattered into the holy river. All of this, I was told, was done to ensure that my grandfather would continue in the cycle of life.

From this day forward, I was troubled by Hindu rituals. I struggled with the idea of worshipping so many manifestations of the gods. I never witnessed any peace, joy, or contentment, no matter how many sacrifices were made. I attended the temple with my family until I was twenty-two years old. Then my father passed away.

My father died on a Wednesday and was cremated on Thursday. As was the custom, someone from each household in the village, irrespective of caste, came to the funeral and paid their respects to my father. Each person carried some wood to add to the pyre.

Once more I had to listen to Vedic hymns dedicated to the sons, the "strong offspring," who eventually would help in lighting a fire. Now those songs were dedicated directly to me. The Hindu priests preferred igniting ritual fires afresh without having to borrow a flame from elsewhere. The fire was usually started by friction, not an easy thing to do. As the only son it was my responsibility to ignite the flame and then set the wood ablaze. I almost refused, but it was a rigid, social custom. My family believed that the final religious rites for parents would not be complete unless a son, preferably the eldest (me), ignited the pyre.

I did not eat, nor did I sleep at all the night after I burned my father's body and raked a large portion of his ashes into the river. I was so frustrated worshipping so many deities and never knowing whether they were pleased with me. My heart ached for truth and knowledge. At 2:30 in the morning I cried out, "I can take this no longer. If there is a God out there somewhere, make Yourself known to me. I will serve You and You alone. I cannot go on like this."

With tears streaming down my face, I walked through the dark house to the kitchen for a drink of water. I took a glass of water and sat on the front porch. As I sat down, the wind began blowing harder than I had ever known it to. As I was about to go inside, I placed my hand on the dirt beside me to support myself when a paper blew up under my palm. I grasped the paper and was about to cast it back into the wind when I noticed the word *God*.

The wind died down as quickly as it had arisen. I sat on the dirt floor of our porch, reading the paper by moonlight. It was a single page, and it told me that Jesus Christ was the Son of the living God. He loved me and gave His life for me (even though He had never met me). There was a handwritten telephone number on the back. I folded the paper up, placed it in my pocket, and went back to bed, wondering about this Jesus.

Later that Saturday morning, I called the telephone number. A man answered, "Jawalakhel's grocery." I slammed the phone down. I did not know how to respond. I took a bus to the grocery store and met the owner, Mr. Rai. I showed him the paper, and he took me to the back room. His face was pale and his hands were trembling as he asked, "Where did you get this?" I told him the story of my struggle and how the wind brought the paper to me.

"This truly must be God's desire then," he muttered.

Mr. Rai told me that he was a follower of Jesus Christ. He gave me a New Testament Bible and told me to read the books titled Matthew, Mark, Luke, and John. Once I completed the reading, I could return, and he would discuss Christianity with me. So I went home and read it in less than a week. It was fascinating. There were stories of Jesus walking on water as well as healing people. Jesus fed over five thousand people with just a handful of fish and bread. He even raised people from the dead. This Jesus must be God, I thought.

When I arrived at the grocery store, Mr. Rai and I walked to his nearby home. After three hours of discussing Jesus, I asked him, "What must I do to be a Christian?" Mr. Rai explained that all I needed to do was to trust in Jesus as my Savior and believe that He was the only true and living God. He explained repentance to me. That evening I asked Jesus to forgive me of my sin and I trusted Him as my Savior. I was twenty-two years old and free at last. I knew that I was free, but I just could not comprehend the depth of my freedom—that would come in the years that followed.

I went to Mr. Rai's home every Monday night to study the Bible. He had been a Christian for over twenty years, and he had more wisdom than anyone I had ever met. The Bible studies would last anywhere from an hour to three or four hours. We went through each New Testament book. We were just finishing up the book of Hebrews when our studies came to an abrupt end. Two years and nine months after my conversion, Mr. Rai was killed in a Maoist attack.

The Maoists are adherents of the Communist system. They have a great disdain for religion, especially Christianity. Due to his Christian influence, Mr. Rai was shot outside his store one evening as he was locking up. Most people believe that he was shot because he refused to support the Maoists, but I believe it was religiously motivated. He had shared the good news of Jesus with a Maoist commander just two months earlier, and it was this commander who led the band who attacked my beloved friend.

After Mr. Rai's death, his wife asked me to help her manage the store. I moved into a flat near the grocery and began helping her. Though her days were long, lonely, and difficult, she managed to keep things together. Two months after I began my career in the grocery business, I began witnessing to Anand, one of our deliverymen. I didn't know that Mr. Rai had witnessed to this man prior to his death. After only four encounters with Anand, he trusted Jesus as his Lord. He told me that Mr. Rai's life was a testimony to his faith in Jesus.

Anand and I began studying the Bible together every Friday evening after the store closed. Anand shared the good news of Jesus with people as he delivered groceries to them. I shared Jesus with people when they gave me the opportunity in the store. One cool, rainy evening, one of our customers caught my eye. There was something special about her, although I was not sure what it was. It was closing time, so I volunteered to assist her with her groceries. I placed one bag under each arm and walked her home.

By the time I arrived at her home, I had mustered enough courage to find out that her name was Kriti, which literally means "work of art." I invited her to my Friday night Bible study. She was curious and she agreed to come. She came to that Bible study and then every Bible study for eleven weeks. We had just finished studying the Gospel of John and were about to close in prayer when I heard beautiful words from her lips: "Wait, pray for me. I want to believe in Jesus too."

That night Kriti became a work of art for the Lord. Anand, Kriti, and I became the closest of friends. We continued our Bible studies, and Kriti regularly brought her friends. Within a year of Kriti's conversion, nine men and fourteen women attended the Bible study. All were believers except for one man and one woman. About that time, I sensed that God wanted me to take our group to the next level. I was convicted that we ought to become a church, like believers did in the New Testament. The group agreed and named me as pastor.

I was the group's pastor for four years, during which we saw sixty-six people come to trust in Jesus Christ and established six more churches in and around Katmandu. As we went on, theological questions began to arise that I could not answer, so I took this as a sign from the Lord that I should enroll in an advanced Bible degree program. Participating in the program required that I move from Katmandu to a community outside of town.

As hard as it was to leave the church, I could not leave Kriti. I loved her. We had dated for several months, and I could not imagine life without her. After intense prayer, I knew what I had to do. I resigned my position at the grocery store and asked Kriti to marry me.

As soon as we were married, Kriti and I left the other believers, trusting that Jesus would provide for us on our new journey. It was truly amazing to watch the Lord at work. Kriti got a job in a bakery the very day we moved into our new home. We lived in an old, two-room house with a concrete floor and a door that would not lock, but we were happy. Two weeks after my studies began, Anand showed up on our doorstep. He said that all seven churches had voted to support me while I was studying the Bible. I was speechless. I had never received money from churches. Anand assured me, "This is God's desire for our churches. Study hard for the Lord and take this money."

When Anand left the house, I unfolded the scarf and coins and bills dropped to the floor. The churches had collected nearly forty dollars. Along with Kriti's income, that would meet our needs for six months. I continued to study and began witnessing in my community. Three months later, Anand appeared on my doorstep once again with twenty-eight dollars. I continued my studies and witnessing.

For some two years, that was the routine. Every three months, Anand would bring an offering, ranging from twenty-eight to fifty-five dollars. During that period, God accepted another twenty-three souls into His kingdom. Kriti and I had started two different Bible study groups, and both had become churches. After two years of intense classes, I graduated with a diploma in biblical studies.

I planned to support my family with a full-time position in a grocery store, but God had bigger plans. The seven churches in Katmandu had grown to 130 believers. Anand asked me to train some of the people to plant new churches. So I began teaching the more mature men from the nine churches—seven in Katmandu and two in our little town—how to share their faith and how to conduct Bible studies. I helped them develop a plan to plant new churches.

The churches continued to support Kriti and me financially. In fact, the offerings increased. Three years after graduation, I insisted that the churches place me on a salary. The offerings had grown to over two hundred fifty dollars a quarter. There now were twenty-two churches with a combined membership in excess of two hundred fifty. I told Anand, "I feel like I am robbing God. Please just give me one hundred dollars a quarter. That is more than enough." We finally compromised with God blessing me with one hundred fifty dollars each quarter. For several years, the Lord continued to bless the ministry with unfettered growth. In a few years, we had forty-one churches and some six hundred believers.

Things were going well until one December morning. I had been preaching in a little house church on the outskirts of Pokhara, not knowing that the Maoists (who are atheists) and the police (who are Hindu) had agreed to plot to kill me. These groups normally are archenemies, and it is amazing how enemies will band together to stand against the Word of God. I had just preached a message on forgiveness, and as I was walking out of the front door, holding my son's hand, two bullets penetrated my chest. One bullet entered just above my heart. The other punctured my right lung. As I fell, two more bullets ripped through my left arm. My five-year-old son, still holding my hand, was crying and screaming. As soon as I hit the ground, I felt the last bullet pierce my left foot. I lost consciousness within a couple of minutes.

I would have bled to death had not a doctor been at the worship service. He responded instantly, taking off his white shirt to bandage my wounds. He went with me to the hospital and removed the two bullets in my chest.

A week later, I regained consciousness in the hospital. After fifteen months of therapy, I could walk, though with a slight limp. I will never be able to use my left arm again. I was later informed that the Maoists had placed two undercover agents in our church network. I trained one of them to plant churches. After the shooting, twenty-six of the forty-four churches were visited by armed gunmen and were told to disband or face the consequences.

Anand and I agreed that the network had to be dismantled. We advised the house church leaders, "You know how to follow the Lord. You do what will honor Him. However, for the safety of your people, have no further contact with us." The relationships were completely dissolved.

In the midst of the dispersion, God has sent even more blessing. Within a few months of the scattering, believers organized a very loose network of 120 churches and 1,250 persons. Since the danger of violence was great, these churches change locations each month.

The persecution has not slowed me down either. Though I speak to church fellowships and gatherings of pastors at every opportunity, God has allowed my ministry to expand into the realm of Christian literature. I am able to train more pastors through the written word. God has protected me and He still amazes me. Every three or four months, an old, dirty scarf still is left on my front porch. Inside I find between forty-five and one hundred twenty dollars.

As I reflect on my life, I realize the purpose of suffering. In men such as Stephen, the first martyr among Christians, we have a beautiful example of how suffering expands the kingdom of God. Indeed, in a recent speaking engagement, I challenged a large crowd to heed the call of God no matter what the cost. At the invitation, more than seventy men publicly committed themselves to becoming shepherds of the flock, knowing that a decision to be a pastor may cost them dearly. In the end, God will honor their obedience with abundant life, a life truly worth living.

CHAPTER EIGHT

FAMILY
The Story of Tamal
(India)

Do not think that I came to bring peace on earth. I did not come to bring peace but a sword. For I have come to "set a man against his father, a daughter against her mother, and a daughter-in-law against her mother-in-law. . . ." He who loves father or mother more than Me is not worthy of Me.
— MATTHEW 10:34–35, 37A

Varanasi, one of the oldest cities of India, is the place of my birth. It is known as "the city of spiritual light," for it is the supposed place where Shiva and Parvati, husband and wife gods of Hinduism, stood when "time started ticking." This ancient city is located on the Ganges River, India's most holy river. It is said Lord Shiva presides over the river and makes it such a holy place. Because of this, thousands of pilgrims come here daily on their spiritual journey.

When I was a young boy, I was expected to submit to all of the gods. In particular, I memorized all thirty-two forms and names of Ganesha, the elephant god and "lord of the hosts." He was to be worshipped first. He is the most worshipped god in all of Hinduism. I was taught that

Parvati, manifested as Devi, Ganesha's divine mother, was the mother of the universe.

Until I was twenty-seven years old, I was surrounded by Hindu worship. My father owned a small icon shop in town near the river, and since Varanasi has thousands of pilgrims daily and is also known as the "City of Festivals," there were always people in my father's shop. I myself worked in his shop from the time I turned eight years old.

At age sixteen, I had progressed to the position of spiritual guide. Daily I wandered through the city's holy sites, making friends with several Hindu priests and holy men. I really appreciated that they spent time with me, so I carefully listened to their teachings. In fact, when I was twelve, I considered becoming a holy man. But that was just a fleeting thought.

In time, I became qualified to lead pilgrims to the holy sites and to explain the historical and spiritual importance of each site. Of course, no pilgrimage is complete without a visit to the bathing ghats since they are a main attraction. I would lead large numbers every day to bathe in the baths and to worship in the temples beside the river. From there, I would take each group to the Durga Temple, which was built in the eighth century. It is one of the most important temples in Varanasi.

No pilgrimage was complete without a visit to the Bharat Mata Temple. This temple, dedicated to Mother India, is one kilometer from the Varanasi station and was built in the Mohandas Gandhi Kashi Vidyapeeth style. Gandhi himself inaugurated this temple in 1936 so citizens could respect the personified Mother India. A large relief map of the undivided India is there, made of solid marble. The mountains, plains, and oceans are shown in accurate scale. Even though I did not make much money in tips from pilgrims, I enjoyed helping them in their journey.

Just before my twenty-first birthday, a friend of my father offered me a position with his company. He was a tour operator that planned trips for tourists from the West. Many of these tourists were Americans and Europeans looking for spiritual wisdom. I worked seven days a week for fifteen dollars each week. That was a great deal of money for me back then. I more than doubled my salary in tips.

Western tourists were different from the Indian pilgrims. Most

Westerners are spectators looking in on Hindu life. Occasionally a true seeker would be part of the group. I would take such a person to one of my priest friends or one of the holy men.

Each tourist to Varanasi expects a unique experience. Each morning, tourists watch the shimmering red and golden reflection on the Ganges at daybreak. Tourists marvel at the high banks, temples, ashrams, and all the pavilions. Each is an experience in itself. Joined with the tranquil beauty are the sounds of chanted mantras and hymns and the fragrance of incense. Mysticism fills the air. Add a refreshing dip in the Ganges with the splashing of water along the ghats, and one quickly understands what it means to find ultimate bliss in Varanasi. That was my life. I introduced people to such experiences.

One day when I was twenty-seven years old, I conducted one of the tour groups to all the sites. This had been my daily life for about seven years. I had earned a great deal of money and had no intention of ever leaving my job. But on this day, I was confronted with reality. As I led the tourists down to the baths, I noticed a man by the river reading a Bible. He was clearly from the West, but his skin was as dark as mine and his hair was jet black. He looked Indian, but he was reading a Bible. I had seen a Bible before, but never by the Ganges.

I was curious about this fellow, so I sat down near him while my group bathed. As I sat down, he looked over at me and asked, "Do you speak English?" At first, I was almost insulted, but then I remembered that many Hindus do not speak English. "Yes, of course I speak English. I am a tour guide," I replied. We began to talk about Varanasi and the Ganges. Somewhere in the conversation, I found out that this man's name was Howard. He was from North Carolina and was part Native American in family heritage. This further intrigued me; an American Indian was in Varanasi, India, reading a Bible. We talked for nearly an hour until my tourists were finished. Howard took my business card, and I went on my way with the group.

That evening I received a call from Howard. He was looking for somewhere to eat. "I want to eat at an authentic local restaurant. I do not want a tourist hot spot. I want to experience real Indian culture. You choose the restaurant, and I will pay for both of us," he insisted. So I recommended a place, and met him there at nine.

The night's experiences were interesting. Howard never mentioned the Bible at all. I was confused because I thought only Christians read the Bible, but Howard was asking questions that were normally asked by true seekers of Hinduism. I did not know how to interpret the signals he was sending. So I asked, "Howard, are you a Christian?" He replied, "Yes, I am." But he continued asking me questions about spiritual matters and Hindu worship. Finally, I asked him, "Do you want to give up Christianity and convert to Hinduism?"

With his reply came the first dose of reality:

> No Tamal, I am not interested in converting to Hinduism. I know several Hindus back home in North Carolina. They are really good people, but they have been deceived. I want to learn as much as I can about their beliefs so I can better understand them. They are my friends and I do not want them to spend eternity separated from the God who so desperately loves them that He actually died for them. That is why I am here.

Something in the tender tone of his voice and the compassionate look in his eyes told me that Howard was genuine. I had just met a real follower of the Bible. I was not quite sure what a real Christian was, but I was sure he was one. Howard and I ate and talked until midnight. During the evening, Howard never expressed to me that I, too, had been blinded by the false teachings of Hinduism. We simply went our separate ways around midnight.

The next day I led another group of tourists to the usual sites, but somewhere in the back of my mind, I thought about Howard. I wished I had another chance to speak with him, but I did not have his phone number, and I was not sure in which guesthouse he was staying. I hoped that he would call me before he departed for home. That evening I did receive a call from Howard. He wanted to go to the university and offered to pay me twenty dollars to guide him for the day. So, I took the next day off, and we headed to the university.

Benaras Hindu University is the oldest and largest university in north India. Its campus covers two thousand acres. It is a great place of education established by the pandit Madan Mohan Malaviya. The term *pandit* is a title given to a revered wise man. Today, the campus has faculties of arts, science, music, Sanskrit, other languages, engineering, statistics, and medicine. On the university grounds is the huge Vishwanath Temple, dedicated to Lord Shiva. It is widely known as the Golden Temple because of the gold plating on its 15.5-meter spire.

Howard seemed truly interested in the temple since it has been visited by all great saints—Adi Shankaracharya, Ramkrishna Paramhansa, Swami Vivekananda, Goswami Tulsidas, Maharshi Dayanand Saraswati, Gurunanak, and others. He spent much of the afternoon speaking with a couple of scholars we met as we entered the university grounds. He asked questions concerning Hinduism that I had never heard before. He seemed interested in methods of sacrifice and views of repentance and the afterlife. Normally, people listened to me speak, but now I listened to Howard.

Later that evening at dinner, Howard asked why I was so quiet. I told him I had been reflecting on the events and conversations of the day. I told him that I had heard about the Jesus of the Bible, but I never heard that He was God. At that moment, Howard removed a Bible from his backpack and turned to the Gospel of John. Within two hours, I believed everything the Bible said concerning Jesus. For the first time, I faced a personal spiritual dilemma.

As Howard and I walked back to his guesthouse, we discussed the claims of Jesus. I knew that I needed to trust Him as my Lord, but there were problems. I would lose my family and home. My parents would be so disappointed that they would force me to move away. I would be fired from my job. My employer was a devout Hindu who would never let a Christian work for him. I wondered if it would be ethical for a Christian to take part in Hindu worship and rituals. I did not sleep that night. I wanted to ask Jesus for forgiveness, but I just could not let go. My fears consumed me.

For two days, I avoided Howard. I led my tours and tried to forget this Bible stuff, but I could not run from the presence of God. I felt like He was chasing after me. The third night I stopped by the guesthouse after work and was told Howard was not in his room. The owner said that Howard was departing for the United States the next day, so I waited for three hours in the guesthouse lobby in order to see Howard.

When he returned, we went to his room. I must have asked a hundred questions concerning Jesus and Christian principles. About 2 AM, I asked Jesus to be my Lord and Savior. With an aching heart and tears streaming, I said, "Jesus, if You can have mercy on me and forgive me for everything I have done wrong, then I beg You to do so. Please open my eyes to all of my sinfulness and I will confess it to You. Please give me courage to face whatever tomorrow may hold. Make me one of Your faithful followers." I meant every word. I wanted to be prepared for the tough road ahead, but nothing except the road itself can prepare you.

Howard and I rejoiced and praised God for another hour, and then I went home. Due to the circumstances, I was only able to get one hour of sleep before I was to go to work. It was not the first sleepless night, but it was surely the most emotionally draining night.

The next two weeks were troublesome as I continued to escort tourists. Things were different. I shared the historical significance of each site but could not bring myself to tell anyone about the spiritual value. I now understood that there was no spiritual value in dead gods who were mere fantasies of man. It only took two weeks before my employer called me into his office. He had received complaints from tourists who grumbled that I seemed ignorant of Hindu beliefs and tradition.

I knew that I had lost my zeal, so I resigned my job and went to work with my father in his icon shop. That only lasted for another two weeks, until I could no longer sell graven images of Ganesha to innocent tourists and pilgrims searching for truth. I could no longer be part of the Hindu deception. I found a job working in a guesthouse kitchen. I cleaned tables, emptied the trash, and washed dishes for thirty dollars a month. I was making less than one-third of my salary as a guide.

After working there for three months, I had to deal with my father. He was suspicious of my actions and he found a Bible hidden under my bed. One night after work, he confronted me. I had never lied to my father, and I was not about to start now. "Father, please understand. I have come to understand real truth. My eyes have been opened to the deceptions of my Hindu beliefs, and I have found truth and life in Jesus Christ," I said.

My father grabbed me by my hair and began to shake my head. At one point, my head hit the table three times. He screamed at me for the first time and told me to "leave my home now." Then he fell back in his chair and began to weep. My mother and two sisters threw my clothes into the front yard. I gathered my clothes from the yard and walked to the guesthouse where I worked. Barid, the owner, had compassion on me and rented a room to me for only forty rupees a day (about one dollar). It was a small room near the kitchen, but it became my home.

Three weeks after my departure from home, I received word that my father had died. As the oldest son, I was bound by Hindu custom to perform funeral rituals. When I approached my parents' home, my three uncles met me at the street. I was told to "go back home. You have no business here. You have betrayed all that is holy, and that is why your father is dead. His heart could not withstand your rebelliousness." I started to turn and walk away but stopped and asked, "May I please see my mother for just one moment? I want her to know that I still love her." My oldest uncle, Amil, struck me in the face with the back of his hand. "Be gone, Christian. Be gone or die," he screamed.

I walked back to the guesthouse and wept for the rest of the day. That night, I prayed to the Lord Jesus, "Jesus, I cannot bear this pain. Everyone thinks that my father's death is a result of my faith in You. I need You to help me. Please send an angel or someone to help me. I cannot do this alone."

For the next two days, I considered suicide. I thought of jumping into the Ganges with a bag of rocks tied around my neck. Maybe drowning would not be so bad. Or perhaps I could jump in front of the bus as it sped down the road, I thought.

But God was faithful. On the fourth day after my father's death, a tourist from New Delhi came to stay with us at the guesthouse. I thought that he was a Hindu, but I learned that he had changed his name from Terak to Matthew when he became a Christian. He went by Matt. Matt and I read the Bible together each day during the week he was in town. I was terribly sad to see him go.

After Matt left, I often wondered if he was sent in answer to my prayer. We corresponded by e-mail after he returned to New Delhi. One day, I received an e-mail that helped me realize that Matt was indeed the answer to my prayer. The e-mail read, "Tamal, look for a letter at the post office. Please respond quickly." Two days later the letter arrived. It said,

Tamal, I have a job for you. I am now the manager of the sports facility at the Crowne Plaza in New Delhi. Take the next bus to New Delhi. I am awaiting your arrival. You will begin as part of my clean-up crew, but I will train you to be a massage therapist. It is a good position. Please come quickly. Enclosed is one thousand rupees (twenty dollars) for the bus fare and expenses.

Barid, the owner of the guesthouse, released me to go to work with Matt. Two days later I was on the bus. I worked for Matt cleaning up the fitness center for just over a year before he sent me to be trained as a massage therapist. We shared a flat together near the hotel and went to church every Sunday. At first, we attended the Church of North India, but later became involved with missionaries who had started a Baptist church.

I now realized God's intention in all that had occurred in my life. The Lord, in His abundant grace, provided a family for me. In placing my faith in Jesus Christ, I had lost my father, mother, sisters, and others. I was ostracized from the people I loved the most. But God gave me a spiritual family with the fellowship of the saints. I realized that I am not alone. I am part of the family of God, a family who cares for me deeply and bears my burdens with me as well.

I never gave up on my own family. I attempted to visit my mother and sisters three times. Each time I was rejected. Then my mother died, without Christ and without hope. Both of my sisters cursed at me when I tried to visit them after the funeral. My oldest sister, Rachana, spit in my face.

While my heart is broken over the blindness of my family, I am forever grateful that God saw fit to open my eyes to the truth. He also continues to provide so much more than I ever dreamed. For the past few months, I have been seeing a woman who is a member of the church. She has only been a believer for about one year. We are praying about marriage. Perhaps God will allow me a family who will honor Jesus. How grateful I would be.

CHAPTER NINE

A Peace That Passes Understanding
The Story of Ashwin
(Sri Lanka)

Repay no one evil for evil. Have regard for good things in the sight of all men. If it is possible, as much as depends on you, live peaceably with all men.
—ROMANS 12:17–18

Sri Lanka is a beautiful mixture of religions, cultures, and races." Tour operators who say such things always direct attention to more peaceful, tranquil images. They focus on similarities among religions and cultures, painting pictures of serene harmony. As a child, I believed the idyllic view. Just before my thirty-third birthday, however, I saw a very different side of Sri Lanka and faced devastating circumstances.

I had seen clashes among Hindus, Muslims, Buddhists, and Christians. They did not involve me. I did not care who or what started the fighting. I just stayed away from the violence. Little did I know that one day it would almost take my life. I should have seen problems coming. I was born a Brahman, the highest of the Hindu castes. Priests and educated persons come from the Brahman caste. I knew the importance of Hinduism to Sri Lankan culture. One could not leave one's caste.

The story of Hinduism's influence on Sri Lankan society began long ago. The Tamils, south Indians who brought Hinduism to Sri Lanka over two thousand years ago, were archrivals with the Buddhist Sinhalese. For centuries, the two groups have waged war with one another, one gaining the upper hand and then the other. The island was visited by Muslim invaders in the twelfth century, Portuguese and Dutch imperialists in the sixteenth and seventeenth centuries, and finally, British colonists by the end of the eighteenth century. The struggle to control Sri Lanka is shown in the religious makeup of the nation. Buddhists are in the majority, but Hindus, Christians, and Muslims comprise 30 percent of the population.

As part of the minority Hindu population, I was expected to hold fast to the beliefs of my religion. Therefore, when I, a Brahman, turned my back on Hinduism and turned to Christianity, I provoked uncertainty. In essence, I was declaring that there is no salvation for Hindus. Why was I siding with another minority religion? I was rejecting my place as part of the "supreme" elite. I was claiming that Jesus is the only way of salvation. This was a serious matter.

I lived most of my childhood in Galle, on the southern tip of Sri Lanka. The port is thought by some to be the biblical port of Tarshish. The best word to describe Galle is "Dutch." The Dutch fort was built in 1663. Its massive ramparts surround the older city. Within its walls stand Dutch houses, museums, and churches.

One Dutch colonial masterpiece is the New Oriental Hotel, built for Dutch governors in 1684. I lived within two kilometers of the hotel. Galle is multicultural and religiously pluralistic. Within my own community, and certainly in neighboring communities, lived people of all backgrounds and faiths. Unlike most Hindus, I made friends with everyone—Hindus, Buddhists, Muslims, and Christians. My father felt differently, taking seriously his status as Brahman. He was holy, at least outside of the home. Someone of a lower caste could not even touch him.

My father constantly scolded me for associating with people of different cultures. When I was twelve, I was whipped with a leather strap for sharing a meal with my neighbor next door, a Hindu of a lower caste. My father thought I was being rebellious. The truth was that I did not want to be lonely and miserable like he was. One would have thought that a Brahman, connected with the "Supreme God," would be happy, but he was the most self-centered and lonely man I have ever known. Contentment seemed to elude my father and his fellow Brahmans. Perhaps that drove me to search for the truth.

When I was twenty, I moved to Colombo. A Muslim friend was manager in a bank and offered me a job. When I arrived in the city, I was spellbound. Colombo was fascinating, a comfortable blend of East and West, past and present. The bustle of the harbor merged with the activity of Colombo's banking and shopping areas. The city's history intrigued me. The original trading settlers were Portuguese, Dutch, and British. One can still see their influence in churches and monuments. Their names, religions, costumes, foods, and even words have been absorbed.

Colombo is Sri Lanka's largest city and my adjustment to its noisy, frenetic craziness was a little hard. I thought that I would never become accustomed to the traffic. The breakdowns that snarl traffic get a shrug and a smile from Sri Lankans. "No problem" could be the national motto. It is certainly the one phrase everyone says each day.

I was a young man living in a new city and working for a childhood friend. My days were filled with new opportunities for learning, but my nights were lonely just as with my father. Perhaps some of my loneliness centered around the knowledge that I was a disappointment to my father. He felt I had betrayed our faith by rejecting Brahman tradition.

I was miserable, so I began my quest for happiness.

I poured myself into my new job. I worked hard and took every opportunity to learn the banking industry. Within six years, I was manager of a new branch office. I had nice clothes, money in the bank, and influential friends. But still I was restless and unhappy.

So I began attending social functions where I would occasionally drink excessive amounts of alcohol. I maneuvered my way into the exclusive private party scene. One of my colleagues rented a warehouse and spent countless thousands of dollars in renovations so he could throw exclusive parties. The "who's who" of society often attended.

I was well liked, and well received in society, yet, I was still empty.

My world changed when the Tamil Tigers, a rebel organization fighting for independence, blew up the Central Bank. I had been working with executives of that bank just hours before the explosion. I quickly realized that life was fragile and temporary. I was forced to admit that one day I, too, would die. I questioned my eternal destiny and its possibilities. I began a spiritual pilgrimage.

For four years, I read all sorts of religious materials. I read every piece of Hindu literature I could get into my hands. I compared Hinduism and Buddhism. I read the Qur'an and studied the "five pillars" of Islam. By this time I was a financially successful, troubled thirty-one-year-old man who was contemplating suicide. I was willing to do anything to find truth and peace. I had transitioned from my search for happiness to a desperate desire for peace.

One day I was having lunch with three colleagues, one of whom was a young woman named Maysa. I assumed Maysa was a Muslim. She was racially Arabic and looked like most Muslim women I had known. At one point during our lunch, the topic of religion came up. Maysa said, "I was born a Muslim, but I was never at peace with myself until I found real truth and peace in Jesus Christ." My jaw must have dropped into my lap. I could not believe my ears. I had never met anyone who had converted from any religion to Christianity. That faith was confined to the West.

At any rate, Maysa's comment sparked my interest, so I asked her if we could have tea together after work. She agreed, and we met that evening. When I asked Maysa about her comment, she spent the next two hours telling me of her struggle to find peace for her soul. "At one point, I considered suicide," she said. Now, that sounded eerily familiar. I had to know more. Maysa and I began to eat lunch together daily. She would read portions of the Bible to me after we had finished our meal. By the fall, I had heard enough. There in the café on the second floor of our office building, I invited Jesus Christ into my life. I became a follower of the Son of God.

I started reading the Bible every night for two hours. At the same time, I stopped attending the elite social gatherings and never took another drink of alcohol from the day I invited Jesus into my life, not even one drop. Finally, I had found peace for my soul. By reading Romans chapter five, I learned what I needed all along was to be at peace with God, and Jesus provided it for me. Life began to dramatically improve. I was content with my life. In fact, near the end of the year, I proposed to Maysa. She agreed and we were married shortly thereafter on Christmas Day. We chose that day because we felt like Jesus had brought us together.

I had not seen my family for over two years. Occasionally, I spoke with my mother, but my father was still hurt that I had forsaken my Brahman status. I wanted my parents to meet Maysa, and I wanted her to meet them. I inherently knew that my parents would not be pleased with my decisions of becoming a Christian and marrying a Christian who was a former Muslim, but I never dreamed that they would react so harshly.

We boarded the Saturday morning train from Colombo and arrived in Galle just after lunch. We hailed a taxi and soon were at the home where I was raised. I was excited to be back. I was hoping that once my family met Maysa, everything would work itself out.

My mother prepared lunch, and the meal was remarkable as usual. My mom is a phenomenal cook. My father was typically quiet. Even though there was a slight hint of tension in the air, it was pleasant right up to the time when I said, "Maysa and I hope that some day we can give you a grandchild. We have decided to raise our children to love and respect Hindu and Muslim tradition and culture. We plan to teach our children to be faithful to the teachings of Jesus and, thereby, love everyone."

My father exploded from the table. His chair flew back some six or seven feet and slammed against the wall. With a voice that thundered as though it had come from the very pit of hell itself, he said, "Out, out, out, you treacherous, wicked ones. Leave now or prepare to meet your God!" I almost fell out of my own chair. My father's eyes were glossed over and as black as coal. It was as if he were not even aware of who he was, and he seemed totally devoid of any feelings.

I grabbed Maysa by the hand and ran for the door. My father began to spew profanities that I had never heard from anyone's mouth before, especially from his. My mother was weeping uncontrollably. Maysa had tears streaming down her face. Her hands were trembling, and she could not even speak. My heart felt like it would explode from my chest, and the only thought on my mind was, "Get Maysa out now!"

We walked for two blocks and caught a taxi back to the train station.

The next train was not due to depart for another three hours, so we waited in the station. Less than an hour later, three policemen entered the station and spoke with the stationmaster. He pointed toward me, and the police walked over to me. "Are you Ashwin?" "Yes," I replied. I was arrested for murder. Immediately following my departure from my parents' home, my mother was strangled to death. My father accused me of the crime.

Maysa wanted to stay with me, but I implored her to go back to Colombo because I knew I would need legal help. Maysa was able to obtain one of the bank's corporate attorneys who had a background in criminal law. It took him three weeks to get me released from jail. I was scheduled for an earlier release, but the night before my release, two guards came to my cell and beat me with clubs and chains. I was charged with additional counts of attempting to escape and attacking a policeman. Those charges were dropped when the police could not produce a battered officer, and I was released.

I was not allowed to return to work until the charges were cleared. I was not fired; I was just in limbo. I knew that Maysa did not earn enough to support us, so I took the only job I could find, working at a fast-food restaurant until my trial date. Within a few months, I was cleared of all charges. The handprints around my mother's neck were much larger than my hands. My father has huge hands, but he was never considered a suspect. He is a Brahman and is above reproach. Even now, it is difficult for me to think that my father was capable of taking my mother's life. And then to think that he placed the blame on me is even more unbelievable.

The police report quoted him as saying, "The Christian killed her. That Christian known as Ashwin murdered his own mother. That is how those Christians are. They destroy all things that are good." I thought that the beating in the police station was bad, but nothing hurt so deeply as watching my father testify in court that he witnessed me strangle my own mother. I thought that I would die. The court almost convicted me of murder based solely on my father's word. The only thing that saved me is that God, in His wisdom, gave me small hands.

I went back to work at the bank the following year. Because of my long leave of absence, I now was a head teller and finance manager of the branch where I had been manager. Late that year my friend asked me to fill his position as general manager over the downtown office.

"Ashwin, in the role of general manager, you will be faced with difficult decisions daily," he asserted. "I am promoting you based on the way you conducted yourself over these past three years. How did you do it? How could you not be bitter with your father? How did you humble yourself to work in a restaurant? You are a better man than me, my friend."

Immediately, I opened up the Bible that was lying on my desk and showed him how we can accomplish all things through faith in Jesus Christ. We began having lunch together every Friday. Within two months, my boss, a Muslim, bowed his knee to Jesus. Now we study the Bible in his home on the first Friday evening of the month. We opened it up to anyone who wishes to come, and we normally have four or five. Occasionally, one of the other vice presidents stops by to listen. Perhaps everyone in upper management will become followers of Jesus.

Though I am able to share the love of the Lord with friends, I have not seen nor heard from my father since that day in court. I heard that he had a stroke, and I tried to visit him in the hospital, but I was met at the door. The nurses refused to let me see him. Trying to find a way to reach him with the good news of the gospel, I sent him a letter last year, but I am not even sure he read it.

On bended knee, I pray to the Lord regularly that my father will see the truth in Jesus Christ. But I can only pray, as all lines of communication are closed. I dream that he will find peace. Maybe God will send a local Christian in Galle to share the gospel. Maybe God will send a tourist to do so. Maybe God will give my father a vision. Maybe he will find peace with God before it is too late.

CHAPTER TEN

A Faithful Father to His Children
The Story of Hastin
(Bangladesh)

Behold, children are a heritage from the LORD,
The fruit of the womb is His reward.
Like arrows in the hand of a warrior,
So are the children of one's youth.
—PSALM 127:3–4

I am tired of all the fighting. In my homeland of Bangladesh, clashes between religious groups have been common ever since Muslims invaded the region more than eight hundred years ago, converting many Hindus and Buddhists to Islam. Later the Muslims were overruled by Portuguese and British, who ruled the region until the twentieth century.

From 1903, both Hindus and Muslims vied for independence from the West, which often led to bitter rivalry between the two faiths. Though independence was finally given after World War II, East Pakistan and West Pakistan were segregated by one thousand miles of Indian subcontinent. After brutal infighting in the country and Indian favoritism toward the East, my country received independence in 1971. We were free to direct our own future.

But the independence of the state did not mean freedom for all people. In the midst of a nation that is over 80 percent Muslim, I was born into a devout Hindu family in Khulna, a stronghold of Hindu population. At fifty years of age, I am tired of all the fighting. For forty-seven years, I was forced to endure the continual onslaught of persecutions from Muslims. Now, as a Christian, I never would have dreamed that my own people, Hindus, would treat me as badly as or worse than Muslims. But, alas, I was wrong.

From my earliest childhood memories, I can remember Muslim attacks on my family, friends, and neighbors for no other reason than their hatred for Hindus. From the time I was six years old, my father must have been dragged from our home and beaten at least ten times. One day, as my mother was walking home from the market, two Muslim men tossed a bucket of dog's blood on her. When she arrived home, blood was still dripping from her face and arms.

Yet, the most heinous atrocity that the Muslims inflicted on my family was when Chandi, my sister, was raped. She was seven months pregnant and four Muslim men, one of which was an imam, broke into her home and violated her. When we attempted to file charges against the men, we were told, "All of you Hindus are liars. A Muslim would never defile himself and touch a filthy Hindu." When Ishan, her husband, returned home, he threatened to kill the four men. For that outburst, he was sentenced to five years imprisonment since one of the men was an imam.

Blind justice seems to elude this Islamic government. Ishan only served fifteen months, but it was difficult on Chandi because she had to move back home and depend on our family to support her and her son for nearly two years. She has never completely recovered from the rape. Every time she sees a Muslim man, she shrinks back. Chandi, who once was so cheerful and outgoing, is now quiet, solemn, and introverted.

Our family was not the only ones to suffer. Islamic violence was a way of life in Bangladesh. Three of the twelve Hindu families in my neighborhood lost one of their family members to Islamic persecution. My next-door neighbor and best friend, Haidar, was beaten to death in the street in front of the police station. There were never any arrests since there were no witnesses, even though five policemen watched the fight.

At one point, the violence was so fierce that the former Prime Minister of Bangladesh, Sheikh Hasina, commanded the Hindu minority to "retaliate against any further attacks of the ruling Bangladesh Nationalist Party." He asserted, "This is your country, your motherland. Irrespective of our religious beliefs, we have liberated this country shedding much blood. You should live here with your full rights." There was retaliation to this statement. Once again, the Muslims were set free and the Hindus were executed or imprisoned. I thought that I had seen it all.

Muslims treated Christians the same as Hindus. A few years back I witnessed six or seven Muslim men break down the front door of a house where a Christian family lived and set it on fire while the family was still in the house. As each family member ran from the burning structure, they were beaten with metal poles. The mother and nine-year-old son died. There was no doubt in my mind that Muslims disdained everyone except other Muslims.

One May, I met John, an American businessman, who shared Christ with me. John's love and passion for Jesus exceeded that of any Muslim or Hindu's devotion to their gods I had ever seen. John and I became close friends. John was married with two children, and I was married with two children. Our families shared a meal at least once a week. When I met John, I was not interested in Jesus. I was interested in John's money. I knew that Americans living in Bangladesh were wealthy, and I wanted a piece of that treasure. However, after about three months I lost interest in wealth. I became fascinated with this Jesus that John kept talking about.

John hired me to translate reports of soil tests and their assessment. I also translated as John trained farmers to improve crop yields. He was amazing. At the end of every training session, he would say, "When it is all said and done, after you have done your best, you must put it in the hands of the Lord. Jesus will never let you down."

John's love and concern for the Bengali people was conspicuous. He was the first Westerner I had ever known who truly cared about us. I quickly discovered that his love was simply a reflection of Jesus living through him. Within a year, I could not resist any longer. I knew that I must know this Jesus just as John knew Him.

John taught the Bible to me, beginning with the four Gospels. By the time we were finished with the gospel of John, my eyes were opened to the truth and I repented of my sin and asked Jesus into my life. I was a new creature. I rejected Hinduism and all of its associated rituals.

My wife, Arya, attended many of the Bible studies and prayed to accept Jesus two weeks after my conversion. Our marriage changed. As a Hindu, I thought of Arya as a piece of property. She was there for my convenience and to meet my needs. Within three months of my conversion, life drastically changed. By reading the New Testament book of Ephesians, I found out that Jesus wanted me to love my wife and treat her the same way Jesus treats the church. So, I began to care for her needs. In a few months, I was madly in love with Arya. I began to teach my children to love and respect their mother. It totally revolutionized our family. Life was wonderful on the inside and on the outside.

Arya, the boys, and I visited her parents, and everything seemed to go well until the evening meal. Our oldest son bowed his head and asked Jesus to bless his food. That opened a discussion concerning Jesus. Arya's parents—both devout Hindus—did not mind us adding Jesus to the pantheon of Hindu gods. However, when Arya told them that as Christians we believed in Jesus alone, Arya's mother slapped her across the face. Her father stood up to do the same. I jumped between Arya and her father and he hit me with his fist. I doubled up my fist and drew my arm back. I was ready to lay him out on the floor, but I heard this soft voice inside my head saying, "I would not hit him. Love those that hate you for My sake."

I apologized to Arya's family for ruining their dinner and hurriedly, we left their home.

Two weeks later, my father, Arya's father, and six other elderly men came to call. These eight wise men came to convince me that I was endangering my family by allowing them to be Christians. The discussion went on until well after midnight. When the men finally left, I thought that I had settled the issue. Four nights later, my father appeared on my doorstep with a Hindu Holy Man. The man had been brought to cast demons out of me. When I refused to let him into my house, the Holy Man cursed me. Life seemed to return to normal until one night when I awoke to the smell of smoke. Our house was on fire. I grabbed Arya by the arm. She would not wake up, so I carried her outside. I ran back inside to get my sons. I could not find my oldest son, so I ran out with my youngest. By this time, fire was consuming the entire house. Fire blocked the doors and windows. I fell to my knees and began to beg Jesus to save my son who was still in the house. At that very moment, I felt a little hand on my shoulder. It was my oldest son. He was alive and unharmed. In fact, unlike everyone else, he did not even smell like smoke.

As I heard his first words, "Papa, why are you crying?" I began praising the Lord. I knew my prayers were answered. When I told my son that I thought he was dead, he said, "No, Papa, the man in white brought me out the back door." I have not found anyone who saw the man in white except for my son. I do not know how Jesus answered my prayer. I just know that He answered it.

Once my house was totally destroyed and the fire was out, we found four canisters of petrol that had been used to start the fire. My neighbor down the street stated, "I saw four men running from the direction of your house before the fire. In fact, one of them looked like your father." The police questioned my father, but no charges were ever filed against anyone. We had lost all our possessions. We were destitute and homeless.

John opened up his home to us, where we lived for four months. One evening as Arya and John's wife were returning home from the market, they were accosted by two men who groped at their bodies. They were not physically harmed, but the harassment was meant to send a message to John and me. The Hindu community blamed John for my conversion. The Hindu community was demanding that we leave town. John tried to relocate his business to another region, but government approval takes time in Bangladesh. It took over six months to get permission to relocate. During those six months, our families were harassed seven times. None of us were hurt, but we were all traumatized by the entire Hindu community.

As soon as we were allowed, John and I moved our families to Dhaka. Once the families were settled, John and I began making two-day trips to nearby communities within a day's drive of Dhaka. We resumed work as usual, but our location was different. As always, the work was going well and all of the farmers loved John. They could tell that he truly did care about them and their families. Our outward lives were at last regaining that peace and contentment we had after salvation.

In my younger days as a Hindu, I experienced persecution from Muslims. In my latter years, I experienced persecution from my Hindu family and community. However, now I would experience persecution from both Hindus and Muslims. John and I would soon feel the extreme wrath of a joint Hindu-Muslim uprising.

It was April, and John and I were returning home from Tangail where we had taught farmers about crop rotation. As we drove past the Skylink Hotel two blocks from our homes, a policeman stopped us. I was dragged from the car and John was told that I was being arrested for arson and that he was to "drive on." When he arrived home, there was a mob in his front yard. Hindus and Muslims alike were looting the remains of his home. His wife and children had been dragged from the home and beaten. All three were rushed to the hospital. His wife and oldest son were soon released and placed in protective custody in dorms at Dhaka University. Every material possession John owned had been destroyed.

The police threw me into a jail cell without charging me with any crime. I believed they were trying to find some way to blame me for what happened to my own family. Two days later, John was allowed to visit me. He gently broke the news, "Hastin, they burned your home again. Arya and the boys are in the hospital. Arya will be out in a few days, but both of your sons are in critical condition." I wept for three weeks until God delivered me.

John hired an attorney to plead my case. Since there was irrefutable evidence that I had been in Tangail for the two days prior to the fire in my home, charges were dropped. At the hearing, the magistrate explicitly let me know, "It would be best for you to move out of Dhaka. You and your type (Christian) are not welcome here. We cannot protect you in the future."

John and his family were forced to leave Bangladesh. Their visas were revoked. Arya was released from the hospital within a week, but it took six weeks for my sons' injuries to heal enough to come home. My youngest son, who is eighteen, suffered nineteen broken bones. Yet, his faith in Jesus is remarkable. He is a strong tower for his Lord.

I am so tired of fighting, but I am truly proud of my two sons when I see the love and compassion that they have for those who have persecuted us. At times, I wish all of the suffering would be alleviated and my sons allowed to live free and happy lives. But what I wish may not be God's best. The Lord, in His wisdom, just might use my two teenage boys to bring revival into the unstable nation of Bangladesh. Perhaps He will bring about a great cloud of witnesses through two young men who tirelessly share their faith in Jesus with those who are their sworn enemies. We all know that such a revival may come at great cost. As weary as I may be, I need to be a faithful father to my children so they, in turn, can see God, the faithful Father, in me.

— PART THREE —

BUDDHIST
PERSECUTION

CHAPTER ELEVEN

A Time of Desperation and Temptation
The Story of Kanya
(Thailand)

*Then Jesus spoke to them again, saying, "I am the light of
the world. He who follows Me shall not walk in darkness,
but have the light of life."*

—JOHN 8:12

Please give me any job. I will work for a little food and a place to sleep at night. There must be something I can do," I cried. I was a twenty-eight-year-old woman, and I was starving. "I will see what I can do," the young storeowner replied. He went into his office and made a phone call. Twenty minutes later, two men arrived in a shiny, black sedan and eyed me from top to bottom. I should have realized something was wrong by the way their eyes examined me, but the man in the store seemed so nice that I assumed his friends were also kind. The older man, Niran, told me that he needed someone to assist him in his work with international clients. I answered that my skills were limited. I could cook and speak English. He seemed sure that I could fit his needs.

I got in the car and went with them to a clothing store in downtown Bangkok. Niran bought me an outfit that cost nearly fifty dollars. He said I could repay him over time. He and his associate took me to a nearby hotel to get cleaned up and dressed. I was instructed to meet them in the hotel restaurant for dinner at 9 PM. The hotel room was amazing, with marble floors and crystal chandeliers. The room must have been twenty-five square meters. The bed had clean sheets, and there was a glassed-in tub and shower. Shampoo and soap were provided. There were even mints on the pillows.

I spent two hours taking my bath. It was heavenly, especially since it was my first time in a hotel and my first bath in four days. Afterward, I put on my new dress and shoes and went down to the restaurant as I had been instructed. When I arrived, Niran was seated with his partner and a Westerner from England. All three men greeted me upon my arrival. This was just too good to be true. It was like a dream. I had never before been treated like this. I noticed that Peter, the man from England, eyed me the same way Niran had earlier. But it did not matter because I was eating for the first time in three days. This was possibly the best meal I had ever tasted.

After dinner, Peter was the first to leave the table. He politely excused himself and thanked Niran for the meal. Then Niran took my hand and looked me directly in the eyes as though he was piercing my very soul. "Kanya, Peter is one of my most important clients. It is time for you to earn your keep. Go up to room 805 and entertain Peter for the evening. Tomorrow morning I will give you fifty dollars, and we will consider the clothes and meal paid for as well," Niran said.

"What do you mean 'entertain' Peter?" I asked.

"Just keep him happy. Do whatever it takes to make him happy. Everything will be fine. Do this for me and I will have you work for me at least once a week. Now go, he is in room 805!" I slowly made my way to the elevator and waited for it to arrive. I prayed that it would stall. I was terrified. I had taken clothes and eaten a dinner for which I could not pay. I was trapped. When I arrived at the room, Peter met me at the door. He was very kind and offered me something to drink, but I refused. We talked and watched the BBC on the television for nearly an hour then he said, "Kanya, come over here and sit by me."

My knees were shaking with nervousness so I could barely walk to the bed. He began to rub my arms with his hands. As soon as he touched my leg, I jumped from the edge of the bed and began to cry. Tears came flooding out. I could not stop. I think that this was the first time Peter had experienced such a display. He did not get angry, but continued asking, "What is wrong? What is wrong?" I told him that I could not do this. When he asked me why, I said, "It is not right. Jesus teaches that only a husband and wife should do such things." I informed him that I had never done anything of the sort before and simply could not because it would not be pleasing to Jesus.

I thought that maybe he would let me go, but when he found out that I had never been with a man before, he offered me one hundred dollars, then two hundred dollars. Finally, he stopped at five hundred dollars. Now my faith was beginning to be compromised. My mind raced with thoughts of what I could do with five hundred dollars. I had not earned five hundred dollars during the last year. I was tempted to take Peter up on his offer and then continue working with Niran.

At twenty-eight years old, I was faced with the dilemma of my life. Just hours earlier, I was homeless, starving, dirty, and hopeless. However, now I was sitting in a five-star hotel in downtown Bangkok. I had just eaten the best meal of my life and there was a man offering me five hundred dollars for a little affection. Some girls in Bangkok do this every day for less than fifty dollars. The temptation was strong, but I had to say no. No matter what Peter said and no matter how much money he offered, it was wrong. Even though I had been starving, cold, and homeless, it was still wrong.

After two hours of crying, Peter told me to leave. He did not seem to be angry, and he promised that he would not tell Niran that I had failed to entertain him. So, at two-thirty in the morning, I left Peter's room. I had no money and nowhere to go, but at least I had been faithful to Jesus.

I was not always in such dire straits. It all began when I committed my life to Jesus. Some people think that following Jesus will lead them to a path of prosperity and wealth. My problems began the moment that I prayed and asked Jesus to change my life.

I had been raised a devout Buddhist. As a young child, I frequently visited Buddhist temples in Bangkok with my parents. My father and mother and all of my grandparents were devout Buddhists. My favorite temple was the Wat Prachetupon at the Grand Palace. Most of the time, we frequented the Wat Saket, which is in the old part of Bangkok.

My father took my mother and me to worship at least once a week. As a *Rua Duen* ("river taxi") driver, he ferried children to school traversing the Chao Phraya River, "the River of Kings." In the evenings, he guided a Hang Yao (long tail boat) carrying goods to the floating kitchens scattered about the Klongs (canals) in downtown Bangkok. I think he loved and was fascinated by Buddhism because he admired the old temples built along the Klongs. Many times, we stopped to admire these stately sites. My father enjoyed stopping and burning incense or purchasing a lotus flower to offer to Buddha.

I enjoyed spending time with my father in the temples, but I never understood Buddhist thought. I admired the Buddha's teaching on good and evil. He taught that our actions should benefit others and not ourselves. I also believed in his teaching on moral justice, that no one escapes the consequences of his own actions. Therefore, those who live their lives filled with unwholesome actions will suffer the consequences of those actions.

The Buddha's teachings on nibbana and nirvana just never made sense. *Nibbana,* which means "to cease blowing," is the ultimate goal of Buddhism. It is known as the third law of truth. In nibbana, suffering and the desire that causes suffering must come to an end, just as the cycle of birth and death has come to an end. *Nirvana* is a state in which one is no longer driven by human cravings and desires.

Yet, none of the Buddhist monks could tell what the state of nirvana was like. Several monks said that Buddha himself was not in nirvana. In Buddhism, there were too many inconsistencies. With animism added to the belief structure, it was just too unbelievable. In spite of my disbelief, I went through the routine of Buddhist worship until I left home at twenty years old.

It was at that time that I first encountered someone who was not a Buddhist. I had been hired at a new bookstore in downtown Bangkok. One day, as I was riding my scooter to work, I had an accident. The accident forced me to spend several days in the hospital recovering from three broken bones. One of my coworkers at the bookstore, Solada, came to visit me three times while I was in the hospital.

We quickly became close friends, going to the movies at the local mall and meeting at Starbucks for coffee nearly every morning that we worked.

One night, just after dinner, I noticed a strange, thick, black book sitting in the chair where Solada normally sat. I picked it up and began to scan it. It was a copy of the Bible—in Thai no less. When Solada entered the room with two cups of tea, I asked her about this strange book. I had never seen a Bible before, and it seemed peculiar to me. As I quickly glanced through its pages, I noticed a story about God creating man and woman. I also read about some leper receiving healing from swimming in a river. In the back of the book there was even a story about these four men riding horses in the sky.

Solada took my hand and explained to me that she was a follower of Jesus Christ. She had been raised in a Buddhist home and was forced to worship a being that was nonexistent, cold, and impersonal. She had met a young Christian man who was different from most young men. This young man was kind, sincere, and never tried to get her to compromise her morals. He shared with her the love of Jesus and gave her a Bible. Solada became a Christian after just two months of reading the Bible. She believed its teachings.

Solada and I talked until the early hours of the morning. That was not unusual. However, we talked about the Bible and how Jesus came to save people from their sin. This was a totally new concept for me. After all, I had never thought of myself as a sinner. The months that followed provided seven or eight more opportunities for Solada and me to read the Bible and discuss the claims concerning Jesus. Nearly a year later, we were discussing a passage from the Gospel of John, "Then Jesus spoke to them again, saying, 'I am the light of the world. He who follows Me shall not walk in darkness, but have the light of life'"(8:12). That night, I realized that I was walking in darkness. I was a sinner, and I needed a Savior.

In tears, I asked Jesus to forgive me for being blind and stubborn. I asked Him to give me the light of life. I left Solada's apartment a changed person. At twenty-one years old, I became a follower of Jesus Christ.

Early the next morning I went to a Christian bookstore to purchase my very first Bible. I took it home and read it from Genesis to Revelation in just under six months. Though I did not understand it all, I understood enough of it to see that it was full of truth. Yet, for those same six months I hid my faith in Jesus from my family. However, things in my life were about to change.

On the night of my twenty-second birthday, I was at my parents' home for dinner when my father asked me what I wanted for my birthday. Without thinking, I blurted out, "Papa, I want you and Mama to become followers of Jesus." Before I could say another word, my father slapped me across the face with the back of his hand. It was the first time I had experienced my father's wrath. I picked myself up off the floor and sat back down in my chair. I asked my father to forgive me for offending him, and he slapped me down again. My mother sat in her chair in unbelief and fear. I crawled to the living room, put on my wrap, and left his home.

My mother came to visit me three times over the next month, but I did not see or speak to my father for almost a year. I continued working at the bookstore and things seemed to be progressing well. Solada and I joined a Bible study group in her building. Five of us girls read the Bible, prayed, and worshipped Jesus together every month. I was still brokenhearted over the way my father had reacted to me, but I had honestly forgiven him.

One night there was a knock at the door. To my surprise, it was my father. I invited him in and we shared a cup of tea. He informed me that I had to stop all this foolishness concerning Jesus or he would force me to move back home. I knew what that meant. Moving back home would force me to embrace Buddhist teachings again. I told him that I loved him and that I forgave him for hurting me, even though he never asked for forgiveness. But I made it clear to my father that I could not move back into my old room because wherever I go, my Bible goes as well.

My father raised his hand as if to slap me, but he stopped in midair. "You will regret your decision. Trust me, it will cost you dearly," he said as he walked out the front door. The next morning I was at Starbucks sharing a cup of coffee with Solada when I caught a glimpse of my father leaving the bookstore where I worked. I thought that it was odd because he had never set foot in that store before. After we finished our coffee, Solada and I walked across the street to work.

As soon as I entered the door, Mr. Putsom took me into his office and notified me that I was being fired. "Your father is an angry and vindictive man. If I do not fire you, he will cause trouble for me and for this store. I am sorry, but you must leave now!" I went home with sixteen dollars in my pocket and no hope of another job.

Later that day when Solada came home from work, she told me that my father had stopped her outside the store after work and threatened her. She said, "Your father knows about the Bible study group. If I have any contact with you, he will make trouble for me at work and for the entire group here. Kanya, I cannot let that happen. I am sorry, but I cannot see you anymore." She wiped tears from her eyes as she spoke. Solada left my apartment that day and never returned. I saw her at Starbucks once, but she sat two tables away and never even acknowledged me. I saw others from my Bible study group, but they too ignored me. All of my Christian friends were afraid of my father; therefore, they refused to even speak to me.

It took me a month to get a new job. It did not pay as well as the bookstore, so I had to move into a very poor neighborhood. Within four months, my father found out where I was working and caused trouble for me. Once again, I was fired. He told the manager that I was a rebellious child and had a history of stealing, all of which were lies. In the next five years, I had eleven jobs and was fired from every one of them due to my father's intrusions. After being fired from my last job, I was penniless. I had no home, no money, no friends, only one outfit of clothes, and my shoes literally were falling apart. No one would hire me, and I could not blame them. That is when I found myself on the doorstep of the small grocery store begging for a job. That is when I found myself saying, "I will work for a little food and a place to sleep." That is also where I found myself nearly compromising myself and my faith for money and the promise of a better future.

Yet, God is faithful even when we are not. Little did I realize that asking for a job in a grocery store would lead to a man's hotel room later that night. I could have never anticipated such temptations. I am so thankful I had learned that the Lord provides a way of escape for those who seek it (1 Cor. 10:13).

Leaving Peter's room early that morning with no money and nowhere to go, I was praising Jesus for providing a way of escape from the temptation. On my way out, I stopped by the toilet in the lobby because I was not sure how long I would be back on the street. A clean toilet is a rare commodity for a street person. As I was about to leave the building, a man stopped me and asked if I had my key.

"I do not have the key and I will not be returning, praise be to Jesus," I said.

The man, one of the hotel's managers, was curious about why I'd said, "praise be to Jesus." I told him my story and he offered me a position as a housekeeper. I let him know about my father's anger and intrusion. He replied, "Let your father talk with me. I will introduce him to our Father. No one can separate us from His care. You just perform your work well. Your job will never be in jeopardy from your father again." I could not believe my ears. This man was a follower of Jesus also.

That night, the manager, Mr. Thiansathaporn, gave me a room to sleep in and allowed me to stay there for one month until I could find a place of my own. The threats from my father ceased altogether. Mr. Thiansathaporn was never approached by my father, so perhaps he gave up on persecuting me.

After two years, I was promoted to assistant head housekeeper, which meant a raise in pay. Within another year, I was head housekeeper and received another raise. Today I manage a staff of thirty-two and love my work. I hold weekly Bible studies in the break room every Wednesday. Ten or twelve ladies usually attend. Eight of them have come to faith in Jesus.

The most amazing part of my story is that one of those who surrendered to Christ was my own mother. She had been coming to the Bible studies for nearly a year. Then one Wednesday evening, Mom placed her hands into my hands and prayed to receive Jesus as her Lord and Savior. At the time of this writing, my father still does not know of my mother's transformation. Knowing how angry he became at my conversion, one can only speculate at the vengeance he might take if he knew that his wife has also become a Christian.

But whatever lies in the future, I am not fearful. A relationship with Jesus Christ is worth any sacrifice. Sometimes late at night, as I lie in bed, I think back and wonder what happened to my good friend Solada.

I tried to find her a couple of years ago, but she had moved and left no forwarding address. The manager of the bookstore told me that she had married, but he did not know the man's name. I know that I will see her in heaven if I do not see her before then. I want to thank her for telling me about Jesus. My decision to follow Jesus caused me a great deal of heartache in the beginning, but He proved His faithfulness in my darkest hours. He delivered me from temptation and set me free.

I never saw Niran after that first night. I hope to see him again some day. I want to introduce him to my Lord.

CHAPTER TWELVE

Not Ashamed of the Gospel
The Story of Nachin
(Mongolia)

To You, O Lord, I lift up my soul.
O my God, I trust in You;
Let me not be ashamed;
Let not my enemies triumph over me.
Indeed, let no one who waits on You be ashamed;
Let those be ashamed who deal treacherously without cause.
—PSALM 25:1–3

History is you and you are history," my father would always tell me. He assured me that, due to my ancestral lineage, I was destined to be a devout Buddhist. My family cared for the Erdene Zuu monastery of Khara-Khorum, Mongolia. Thus, every corner of my world was immersed in Buddhist history. I wondered how history could control every aspect of my life. By the time I was twenty-four years old, I could no longer follow the path and religion of my forefathers. I thought, "I will just walk away." But I wasn't sure what I was walking away from.

Chingis Khan built Khara-Khorum in 1220 as capital of the Mongol Empire. His son Ogodei Khan completed construction on the city, but the government soon moved to Beijing as the dynasty expanded. Khara-Khorum essentially was abandoned. The Erdene Zuu monastery, the first Buddhist monastery in Mongolia, is the only remnant remaining from this once great city. The monastery, surrounded by a stone wall and 108 stupas (Buddhist shrines), is a reminder of Buddhist prominence and a memorial to the religion. At its height, one thousand monks and nearly one hundred temples were within this monastery. Today, the monastery is home to some of the world's most important religious scripts. Mongolian, Chinese, Arab, and Tibetan scripts of the thirteenth and fourteenth centuries have been preserved in the temples. The central plaza of the monastery, forty-five meters in diameter and paved with flagstones, in English would be called "the Square of Happiness and Prosperity." This is the history my family holds so dear.

As a young boy, I listened as my father told stories of how he and my grandfather fought to protect the monastery from thieves and robbers. I would go with my father to worship in the different temples regularly. He was faithful to teach me the Dharma (teachings of Buddha), and he was diligent in showing me how a good Buddhist should live. My father is the greatest example I have ever known of someone who truly tried to live by the teachings of the Buddha. I deeply admired the Buddha for some of his great teachings. I especially liked the principle of nirvana. From my earliest memories, I strived to be a good Buddhist like my father and grandfather.

Things changed, however, when at twenty-two years of age I moved to Ulaanbaatar, the capital of Mongolia today. My father sent me to Ulaanbaatar to work with my uncle in the spice market. Every day we would haul one hundred kilos of assorted spices into the market by horseback. Then we would separate the spices to sell. My uncle paid me twenty-five dollars per week plus gave me room and board. Since my father had become invalid, I sent eighty dollars home each month.

I worked seven days a week, but at night I would meet two friends, Baiju and Sukh, for tea and conversation. One night not long after I arrived in Ulaanbaatar, Baiju introduced me to Samuel, an exchange student from America who was studying language, culture, and politics. I quickly became friends with Samuel. I noticed something in him that I admired deeply. Samuel seemed to live life with passion. He was a Christian, and quite an intriguing individual. I had heard about Christians, but Samuel was the first one I had met.

I tutored Samuel in the Mongolian language, and Samuel taught me to speak and read English. Often I read from the Bible to him to test my English skills. I usually commented on how the teachings of Jesus were similar to the teachings of Buddha. After inquiring as to why I thought they were parallel in their teachings, Samuel would gently explain the differences to me. After studying three nights a week for ten months, I asked Samuel, "Can I become a Christian? These teachings of Jesus seem to be a better way of life."

Samuel broke my heart when he informed me, "Nachin, my friend, you cannot become a Christian. A Christian does not live his life because it is a better way. A Christian follows the teachings of Jesus because Jesus is God." This was a new concept. I thought that Samuel had had some type of mental lapse. "Jesus is what?" I replied. Samuel took me to the passages of the Bible where Jesus claimed to be God. Things began to make sense, and everything fell into place. Samuel was right. Buddha simply claimed to be a good man with good teachings, but Jesus was different. He was God. That night in Samuel's little flat, I prayed to receive Jesus Christ as my Lord and Savior. I realized that Jesus was not merely a better way; He was the only way.

I hid my decision from my Uncle Tolui, because I knew that he would tell my father. Moreover, I could not stand the thought of my father being disappointed in me. After all, I was destined to be a good Buddhist who would help preserve its history. I continued working days with my uncle and studying the Bible with Samuel three nights a week. This worked well until six months later. My aunt found a Bible in my backpack. She told Uncle Tolui, who exploded in anger.

We did not speak for three days. Finally, I told him about my decision to be a follower of Jesus. Before I could finish my sentence, Uncle Tolui hit me in the face with the back of his hand. It was more a slap of disgust than an attempt to hurt, or so I thought. Later that evening, two policemen arrived at our home. Uncle Tolui let them in and pointed to me. There is no law prohibiting a Buddhist from converting to Christianity, but the police were there to escort me out of my uncle's home.

I took the bus back to Khara-Khorum. My father met me at the door and abruptly asked if it was true. "Have you abandoned the teachings of the Buddha?" he inquired. As gently as possible, I explained all that I could about Jesus. My father listened intently and then proceeded to curse at me. At twenty-four years old, this was the first time I ever heard such words from my father's lips. I was shocked. Then he sternly said to me, "Leave, son, just leave. You can no longer live here."

That night, I slept behind the shed in the back yard. The next morning my father had me arrested for trespassing. Normally that would be a small fine; however, my father thought that he could pressure me into, once again, believing the Dharma. I spent the next forty-five days in jail. Every day, the police chief would say, "Nachin, forget these teachings of Jesus, and you can go back home." I must admit that I was tempted, but I knew that Jesus really was the Son of God. I also knew that Buddhism was a dead religion. I could not recant my faith. Jesus was too real.

Upon my release from jail, my father met me. Without saying a word, he gave me thirty-five dollars and turned his back on me, as if to say, "We are finished." I will never forget that heartbreaking night. I slept outside the bus station. Early the next morning, I took the bus to Ulaanbaatar to visit Samuel. He offered to let me stay in his flat. I quickly accepted.

Samuel told me about a position at the university landscaping and caring for the grounds. The pay was about the same as my uncle had given, so I began saving enough to move out on my own. I worked six days a week and studied the Bible nearly every night. Samuel showed me things in the Bible that astounded me. I loved to read about Jesus walking on water and calming the storm. The Bible seemed to come to life more with each reading. I could not put it down.

One day at lunch, I was reading my Bible when Tipu, a coworker, noticed that I had a Bible. I began sharing the good news of Jesus with him. Within two weeks, he too became a follower of Jesus. The two of us decided to meet every Tuesday night for Bible study and fellowship. Occasionally, we would invite others. Eventually, I moved into my own flat and began to share with more people. At the end of our first year, nearly twenty people attended regularly and seven became followers of Jesus. Things were going so well.

One evening, as we were about to begin, there was a knock at my door. When I opened the door, eight policemen dressed in paramilitary gear rushed in. Two of them pressed my face into the concrete floor so hard that it broke my nose. Everyone was arrested and taken to jail. We were all placed in separate cells and not allowed to speak to anyone. I was detained for three days before I was allowed to speak to the police chief.

I had been charged with the proselytizing of Buddhists, which evidently was a crime. I was kept in solitary confinement for ten weeks and then transported to a reeducation center. I was forced to study the teaching of the Buddha every day for nine hours and to meditate for six hours. The reeducation process was scheduled to last one month. I was there nearly a year.

I thought I would go crazy. Every night I would beg Jesus to either take my life or free me. After the first two months of indoctrination, I just could not take it any longer, so I began quoting Scripture during the meditation time. That comforted my soul for several months. However, one evening I got carried away and began singing a song that Samuel had taught me: "Oh victory in Jesus, my Savior forever—." A rifle butt came smashing down on my head.

I awoke several hours later in the hospital. I had a severe fracture, and had lost a liter of blood. During the first five weeks of my hospital stay, I was not allowed to receive visitors. Finally, one evening, Tipu showed up by my bedside. He reported that the police had killed one of the young men who had been arrested at my home a year earlier. Supposedly, he was shot in the back "while trying to escape." His body was never released to the family.

Tipu told me I was in grave danger. He also had been sent to a reeducation center. After two months, he decided to deceive the teachers and agreed to follow the teachings of the Buddha. He was allowed to reenter society.

He warned me that I had only two choices. I could recant my belief in Jesus and reenter society as a Buddhist, or I would end up like my friend, shot in the back. I told Tipu that I could not renounce the Lord Jesus who had died for me and if need be, I would die for Him. I began to pray harder than I had ever prayed before. I fervently prayed, "Jesus, give me strength to endure. Please do not let me deny you."

Two days later Tipu paid me another visit. He and Samuel had been talking. They had devised a plan of escape. That night, Tipu helped me slip down a back staircase while the nurse was eating dinner. I hid under a blanket in the back of Tipu's taxi. As we stopped at the checkpoint, I trembled as the guards were searching the vehicle. The guard checked the car thoroughly. He checked every inch, but he never noticed me under the blanket. I believe that the Lord simply blinded him to my presence. Jesus had provided a means of escape.

Tipu and I were now on the run. We stayed with Samuel that first night, but we had to leave Ulaanbaatar. Tipu's mother, who had also become a Christian, arranged for Tipu and me to stay with a family member in a nearby village. We stayed for two months, until the local police began to ask questions about us.

We quickly were moved to some family friends who lived in the Gobi Desert. We lived in a Yurt, a round tent covered with animal skins, with a family of six. After six months, Tipu and I moved to Dalandzadgad and found jobs in the local market. Once again the police began to inquire of us. Finally, we fled to the mountains and crossed the border into China.

I was forced to leave my beloved homeland and heritage behind. I have become the personification of the New Testament word *pilgrim*. Like many Jews of the Old Testament and Christians of the New Testament, I have experienced exile from the land of my fathers because of my faith. I am now a stranger in a strange land.

Gone are the days of my childhood when my father had great hope that I would protect the faith as had so many of our ancestors. Gone is the expectation that I will stand alongside my ancestors as warriors for Buddha, protectors of the great monastery.

In one sense I stand alone. No mother. No father. No family. No heritage. No history. Yet, I have so much more. I am surrounded "by so great a cloud of witnesses" (Hebrews 12:1), and I stand proudly on the truth found in Jesus Christ. I may not have a family who is proud of my actions, but I have a heavenly Father who will never leave me nor forsake me. Ultimately, He is all I need.

For now, Tipu and I work in a small town near the Mongolia border. I am a fugitive in my homeland. My prayer is that someday I can return home, not so I can enjoy my homeland again, but so I can proclaim to my father and mother that Jesus loves them, died for them, and wants to forgive them. I don't want them to live for history. I want them to live for eternity.

CHAPTER THIRTEEN

Downtrodden but Delivered
The Story of Tai
(Cambodia)

*We are hard pressed on every side, yet not crushed; we are
perplexed, but not in despair; persecuted, but not forsaken;
struck down, but not destroyed—always carrying about in
the body the dying of the Lord Jesus, that the life of Jesus
also may be manifested in our body.*
—2 CORINTHIANS 4:8–10

Fear dominated my life from early childhood through my late twenties.
I grew up under the tyranny of Pol Pot and the Khmer Rouge, a regime
that killed some 2 million Cambodians during the 1970s and 1980s. As
a young child, I stood outside a schoolhouse, which today is a genocide
museum, and watched the Khmer Rouge cut off my father's fingers one
at a time. They began by cutting off the fingers at the first joint and then
moved down the fingers joint by joint. The process took over a week to
complete. I can still hear his screams echoing down the hallways and
out of the windows. He was tortured for nearly two weeks before he finally died. His crime was that he was educated. My father was a devout

Buddhist and an excellent teacher. He taught economics and religion in the local high school near our home in Phnom Penh.

After my father's death, my mother, sister, and I moved to Angkor to live with my grandparents. I was quite relieved to be out of Phnom Penh and away from Pol Pot, or so I thought. At first I enjoyed living with my grandparents, but the peace and serenity soon ended. The Khmer Rouge took my grandfather, and he, too, was killed within three months. During that time, I was forced to worship at a different Buddhist temple every day, and some days we went to multiple temples. My grandmother and mother became convinced that if I were to become a Buddhist monk, then it would appease the Buddha. In return for our devotion, he would intervene and spare my grandfather's life. But the Buddha had no effect on Pol Pot and did not intervene for anyone to stop the reign of his tyranny.

After my grandfather's death, I remained a monk. I was committed to a minimum of two years of service as a novice. During those years, I became enthralled in the Buddha's teachings and swiftly took the vow of a monk. During eleven years as a monk, I became quite educated. By the time I was twenty-five years old, I could speak and read Khmer, Vietnamese, Thai, and English. Under Pol Pot, that was rare and dangerous knowledge.

I studied and practiced Theravada Buddhism, called the "doctrine of the elders." These teachings come from the school of Buddhism that draws its scriptural inspiration from the Tipitaka, or Pali Canon, which scholars generally agree contain the earliest surviving record of the Buddha's teachings. I was diligent in studies and excelled.

The goal of a follower of Theravada Buddhism is to become an *arhat,* a sage who has achieved nirvana enlightenment. This person seeks to leave the cycle of reincarnated birth and death and no longer be reborn. Even though I knew that reaching nirvana was not possible, I sought to achieve it anyway. By the time I was twenty-seven years old, I was teaching in the temple. I had reached a level at which I could be considered in some circles a scholar or professor of Buddhism. But my life still seemed empty and hopeless. I had achieved more enlightenment than most men twice my age, but I was spiritually empty and terribly lonely.

Angkor has many temples, and because of their beauty it is a hot spot for tourists. I met an American who had come to Cambodia on holiday. He was taking a tour of the temple and I heard him say, "What a pity to see so many people being blinded by Buddhism."

"Blinded? What do you mean 'blinded'?" I asked. The man introduced himself and began telling me about the false teachings of Buddha. I became angry and defended every point of contention with vigor and passion. However, deep inside I knew that the man was speaking the truth. I knew that Buddhism was a dead and useless religion. Buddha was dead and that was all there was to it.

Just before the American left the temple, he asked me to forgive him. When I asked why he needed forgiveness, he replied, "Forgive me for the manner in which I spoke of your faith in Buddhism. I was too harsh toward you. I just wanted you to know that all religions are empty and vain. I had hoped to show you that true everlasting life can only be found in a genuine relationship with Jesus Christ." Then he placed a little book in my hand and turned away. He had given me a copy of the New Testament, translated into both English and Thai.

That night during my meditation time I began to examine this gift. I read all of Matthew in one evening. The stories of Jesus intrigued me so much that I read all four Gospels within a week. The stories were just stories to me, but somehow they were different than the stories I had read about Buddha. These narratives seemed to ring true. I believed them.

Within a month, I had read the entire New Testament. Some of the teachings seemed strange, but I believed what I could understand. I needed someone with whom I could talk about my thoughts, so I went to speak with the highest figure in the temple. If a comparison could be drawn, he would be the equivalent to a New Testament Pharisee. Although he interpreted the teachings of Buddha, he had also read the teachings of Jesus as well as Muhammad. Thus, I sought him out for wisdom.

Immediately, he chastised me for even reading the Bible. I had been a monk for ten years, yet I was forced to perform the duties of a novice for six months. My only crime was that I had become curious about Jesus and His teachings. My Bible was burned and I was disgraced in front of my peers. I was not allowed to leave the temple alone. I was escorted everywhere during my six months of punishment.

Now I was so disillusioned with Buddhism and its emptiness that I prayed nearly every night to God. "If these things about Jesus are true, then send someone to explain them to me," I pleaded. This was my prayer for six months. After the end of my period of punishment, I was sent to Wat Ounalom and Wat Phnom in Phnom Penh for reeducating.

I was in the reeducation process for just over a month when I decided to turn my back on Buddhism. I turned in my orange robe and denounced Buddha and his teachings. The two months that followed were remarkably peaceful. No one from the Wats approached me nor did they threaten me in any way. Yet, things changed quickly after my conversion to Christianity.

Upon release from my Buddhist vows, I began work in the secular realm for the first time in my life. Mr. Sing, a devout Buddhist, hired me to work in his scooter store. My first day on the job I met an American named Paul. He had come in to the store because his rear tire was worn and needed to be replaced. I told him that the tire would cost him twenty-four dollars, so he had me replace it. When the owner returned from lunch, he let Paul know that the tire would cost forty-five dollars.

I was embarrassed that Mr. Sing, a devout Buddhist, was overcharging Paul because he was an American.

Even so, Paul simply paid the higher price without complaint, smiled, and said, "Thank you, Tai. You did a wonderful job installing my tire. I hope I see you again." Then he drove out of sight on his scooter.

One evening two weeks later, I saw Paul at the park down by the Mekong River. He greeted me, and we shared a cup of tea from one of the street vendors. I was immediately drawn to Paul. Sent to Cambodia by an American agricultural firm, Paul taught the Khmer people how to be better farmers. He was a soft-spoken man with such a gentle spirit that I was intrigued by him.

As we were leaving the park, I apologized to Paul for Mr. Sing's greed. "Tai, do not concern yourself," he said. "The Lord has always taken care of my needs. I am not angry with you or Mr. Sing." He then explained to me how Jesus forgave people who mistreated Him, and Jesus instructed His followers to do the same.

That night when I went home, I prayed to God again, "If Jesus is real, I beg you to show me." At that instant a powerful thought went through my head: "How much more convincing do you need? I sent my servant Paul to show you that My Son is real." It was a thought so powerful that it seemed almost audible.

The next day Paul came by the shop with a flat tire. It was his front tire, so we replaced it with a new one. Once again, Mr. Sing charged him forty-five dollars. Paul invited me to have dinner in his home. I had never even dreamed of being in an American's home. I agreed, and that night I rode my scooter to his home.

His home looked like most Khmer homes. It was not extravagant at all. I was treated to American hamburgers and French fries, a real treat. After dinner, we sat on his back patio and sipped tea. Paul took out a Bible and asked me if he could tell me a story. I told him I had read the entire New Testament, and I would be happy to listen to his story. As he began, he asked if I had any questions about my readings in the New Testament.

I had several concerns, but my primary concern was about Jesus's death. "If Jesus was God and never committed a sin, then why did He have to die?"

Paul took the next three hours explaining to me how it was all part of God's plan to redeem humanity because humanity could not redeem itself. After his explanation, I told him that I had been a Buddhist monk and had denounced Buddha only a month before because I realized that Buddhism was a dead religion. Then I added, "But today, I denounce all gods. There is only one, true God and He is the Jesus Christ of the Bible. I will live by His teachings for as long as I live. Can you help me get a Bible?"

With tears on his face, Paul led me in a prayer that stated to God that I turned from my past sins and accepted Jesus as my Savior. Paul wrote an inscription in the front of his own Bible and handed it to me. The inscription said, "To Tai, my son in the faith. Live by the words of this book and you shall be eternally blessed." Now I had tears; Paul had called me his "son" and had given an expensive American Bible to me. The next day I went with Paul to the International church. People were singing and clapping their hands. Some were standing and praying to God. It was so different from anything I had experienced that I was too distracted to really worship on that first Sunday.

On the way out of church, I encountered my reeducation teacher. He had not seemed concerned when I recanted my Buddhist vows, but he was visibly disturbed that I could be seen coming out of a Christian church. He scolded me in public and slapped the Bible out of my hand.

I had been studying the Bible with Paul for just over a month when I was attacked outside my home. I was arriving home from work late one night when two men with four-foot-long iron poles attacked me. Blood spattered my front porch and it looked as though it was sprayed solid red. My neighbor helped me into the house. Since I did not have a telephone, my neighbor walked to Paul's home for assistance. Paul took me to the hospital on the back of his scooter. I almost fell off because I was in and out of consciousness.

Three days later I was released from the hospital and went back to work. Mr. Sing was very understanding concerning my injuries, but two weeks later I was fired. The chief leader from Wat Phnom paid Mr. Sing a visit and instructed him to fire me. Mr. Sing expressed to me, "Tai, I have never seen a harder worker than you, but you must forget all of these lies about Jesus or I will be forced to fire you."

Suddenly, I began to panic. My mind was racing in an attempt to think of what I might say. My heart was pounding so hard that I thought it would burst. Sweat began rolling down my face and dropping to the floor. What was I to do? I had no other prospects for a job. I had no money to live on, and I was even hungry at that very moment.

But I just could not reject Jesus. It seemed like an eternity as Mr. Sing waited for my response. Finally I broke the silence and said, "Mr. Sing, thank you for allowing me to work with you. You are a wonderful man and I deeply respect you, but I cannot denounce Jesus. He is the only true and living God. He died for me, and I just cannot forget that He loved me that much. If you must fire me, then I will leave in peace."

Tears began to roll down Mr. Sing's face. He reached inside his right pocket and pulled out some money that had been folded inside. "I am truly sorry, but you must go now," he replied as he handed me the folded money. I tucked it into my shirt pocket and walked down the street. He had given me nearly seventy dollars.

That night, I went to Paul's home for Bible study. When I informed him of my dilemma, he shouted, "Praise the Lord. God has answered my prayers." I thought he was crazy. I was in pain, and Paul was praising God. He explained, "Tai, I have been praying that the Lord would provide me with an assistant. I need a national to translate for me. I wanted to have a Christian translator so I could share Jesus with my Khmer colleagues. Praise the Lord for He is good."

For the first year of my new job, things went extremely well. Paul paid me sixty-five dollars a month over what Mr. Sing had paid. He bought me a very nice used scooter since Mr. Sing kept the one he let me use when I worked for him. I loved translating once I learned the agricultural terms. I became proficient in business and as an evangelist. Paul and I led two of his colleagues to faith in Jesus.

One evening as I returned home from work, two men forced their way into my home as I was opening the front door. I was instructed to lie on the floor face down and to keep silent. The two men gathered up every piece of Christian literature and then began to whip me across the back with cane poles. This went on for about ten minutes, until my back was covered with welts and blood. Then one of the men, whom I recognized as the brother of the chief leader, declared, "Deny Jesus or you can die with Him!"

When I refused to disavow Jesus, they poured hot liquid on my freshly beaten back. I thought that I would die at that moment. I screamed in pain and the two men ran. Another neighbor came to my rescue. She ran to Paul's home and returned with him. Paul rushed me to the hospital. I learned that the men had filled my wounds with a mixture of petrol and poison. Had Paul arrived an hour later, I would have died. Two days later, upon my release from the hospital, Paul asked me to move into his home.

As I tell you this, I have been living with Paul for two years now and there have been no more attacks. Occasionally I will see someone from one of the monasteries who knows me. They give a hard look, but I can endure that too.

Reflecting on my life since I trusted Jesus, I have wondered why I had to face persecution. Yet, God has used my experiences to bring people to faith in His Son. For example, both of the neighbors who ran to Paul for help when I was in trouble have become followers of Jesus. Observing how I reacted to the attacks, they testified, "I must have your kind of faith."

I am most thankful that my former boss and good friend Mr. Sing trusted Jesus just a few months ago. I took my scooter to him for repairs. When he questioned me about my strong beliefs in Jesus, I shared the story of Jesus on the cross and asked him, "If that is not love, then what is?" Praise the Lord that he, too, became my brother that day. In fact, he gave me two new tires, a tune-up, and a full tank of petrol to show his gratitude that I had simply shared the good news with him.

I never wanted the beatings, mocking, and rejection. But if this is what it takes to wake a sleeping world that is hopelessly traveling toward a Christless eternity, then so be it. If my life needs to be an example of victory through suffering, I will gladly submit to God's will. For I am fully aware that the greatest love ever demonstrated to humankind came through the greatest suffering ever endured by a man. It is by His stripes that we are healed.

CHAPTER FOURTEEN

The Sufficiency of Scripture
The Story of Aran
(Macau)

*Then he said, "I beg you therefore, father, that you would
send him to my father's house, for I have five brothers, that
he may testify to them, lest they also come to this place of
torment." . . . But he said to him, "If they do not hear Moses
and the prophets, neither will they be persuaded though one
rise from the dead."*
—LUKE 16:27–28, 31

Macau, a minute territory on the southern coast of China, has a rich
European history forgotten by most Westerners. This semi-autonomous
region, handed over by the Portuguese to the People's Republic of China
in 1999, is a distinctive blend of the past and the present. While casi-
nos and hotels dot the landscape of this province's twenty-two square
kilometers, Baroque Roman Catholic churches and ancient Buddhist
temples also are noteworthy. But the influence of the Chinese government is becoming more prevalent. At this writing, the majority of the
half million people who call Macau home are Buddhists, and more than
10 percent are Catholics. But an increasing number hold to the Party
line of atheism.

China had too much influence in our lives even before we were handed over to them. When I was a young man, China gave us a glimpse of what we could expect. Beijing has long arms and began to tighten her grip on my life. Not many eligible females were available to become brides. To solidify Macau's connection with the mainland, China shipped young women into Macau from different regions to provide more suitable brides. I know because I married one of them.

At age twenty, I was introduce to Lei. I fell madly in love with her immediately, and we were married within a month. Only then did I discover that she had been stolen from her home in Chungsha and sent against her will to Macau. Two weeks after our wedding, she told me that she had been abducted on the street and transported on a bus with thirty other kidnapped women. It was reported that the Chinese government paid the kidnappers one thousand two hundred dollars for each kidnapped woman. She cried as she said, "My family will be killed if I return to China. I was told that Mother China needed me to insure her future here in Macau. I can never go home." She wept continuously for days. It took nearly a year for Lei to begin to love me. Broken by the tragic situation, I assured her that some day I would take her home to visit her family.

For the next eight years, Lei and I worked in a textile mill while we attended the university at night. After graduating from the University of Macau with a degree in business, I was hired by the Macau Department of Transportation. Lei went to work as an accountant for a hotel chain. Our years of hard work and study had paid off. We could begin to enjoy our life together.

That fall, I was assigned to work at the ferry terminal, which was home to a fleet of high-speed vessels that served the forty-mile route between Hong Kong and Macau. Within a year, I was qualified to pilot jetfoils, turbo-cats, jumbo-cats, and hover ferries. I became close friends with Zirion, my Portuguese copilot. Zirion actually moved into my spare bedroom for well over a year.

During that year, I noticed that Zirion was different from all of my other friends. Most of my friends were Buddhists. They, like me, observed the traditional Buddhist festivals and ceremonies. We were definitely consistent in our observance of the rituals, but we were not faithful to

Buddhism in our daily lives. Buddhism seemed an irrelevant religion to which we were expected to adhere according to ancient traditions.

But Zirion took faith in Jesus Christ seriously. He would not drink alcohol, nor would he participate in any activity that he considered contrary to the teachings of Jesus. I had never met a man of such convictions. Zirion observed the teachings of Jesus in his everyday life. I had to know more about this Jesus whose teachings were so influential.

Eventually, I asked Zirion to teach me about Jesus. We decided to begin with reading the Bible two nights a week for two or three hours at a time. Due to the profound material, on occasion we studied for five or six hours. One night, we studied from just after dinner until three in the morning. Needless to say, I was glad that I was not driving the jumbo-cat the next morning. I was exhausted, yet my mind was filled with so many questions.

That fall, after more than six months of Bible study, I was convinced of the claims of Christ and invited Jesus into my life. I told Lei of my decision, and she shared with me that she had become a believer two months earlier. She had been waiting for me to make my decision before informing me of her commitment. Lei and I were excited that we had finally found the truth. Moreover, God, through His Word, gave us divine guidance on our marriage and how to honor Him with our love for each other.

We joined a Cantonese-speaking church near our home and felt right at home. When the pastor agreed to baptize us on Lei's birthday in October, we were thrilled and decided to invite my parents to the baptism. The very day that the pastor agreed to baptize us, Lei and I went over to my parents' home. Upon hearing of my conversion, my mother wept for two hours. My father tried to reason with me into the early hours of the next day. At about 2 AM, he lost patience and demanded that I leave his home. He condemned me as a disgrace to the family and to the Chinese people. "You have been too close to that pagan Portuguese who lives with you. I wish you were dead. It would be better for the family," he said.

Lei and I left my parents' home and prayed all the way home that God would open their eyes to the truth. We were baptized two Sundays later in a stone pond beside our church. When I came up out of the water, I was shocked to see my mother standing in the midst of the congregation.

Once I was dressed in dry clothes, I immediately went looking for her. I could not find her. Lei notified me later that she had watched as my mother walked down the hill toward her home. I was happy to see my mother at my baptism, but it was bewildering. My mother never went against my father's wishes.

My father did find out that my mother had come to my baptism. He was furious. He called her a traitor and friend of the evil one—meaning me, I think. When my mother refused to apologize, he packed her clothes in two garbage bags and threw them into the city waste disposal. Then he exclaimed, "If you love that wicked son of yours, go to him! You are not welcome here anymore." After forty-one years of marriage, my father threw my mother out of the house. Of course, Lei and I gladly opened our home to her.

After two months, I thought that surely my father would be missing my mother and would be a bit more rational than the last time I had spoken with him, so I paid him a visit.

He met me at the door with a smile on his face. "Come in," he said in a calm, pleasant tone. As I entered the living room, I saw that I had interrupted a meeting between my father and five of his closest friends, one of whom was a former Buddhist monk. I was forced to sit on the floor surrounded by these five men and my father and listen to them threaten Lei, my mother, and me. They had been drinking wine and were intoxicated. No wonder my father was so pleasant when he greeted me.

I listened to them for nearly two hours. When I tried to stand up to leave, my own father pinned my left hand to the floor with his foot. Ek, the former monk, pinned down my right hand with his foot, and the other men beat me in the face and chest. The beating must have lasted for at least fifteen minutes.

I awoke the next morning just before daybreak lying in the trash bin behind an American fast food company's restaurant. I pulled myself out of the trash and walked to the hospital. I had three broken ribs, a punctured lung, and a fractured left arm. I called Lei from the hospital. My father also had visited my house while I was lying in the trash pile. He tried to get my mother to go home with him. She refused because she could tell he had been drinking and sensed that he wanted to hurt her.

When I returned to work nearly a month later, I was told Zirion had been fired and that I was on probation. When I asked the reasons I was told that several different men had made allegations against us. Zirion had been found guilty and I was still under investigation. One of my father's friends works for the port authority and his brother is one of the senior chiefs in the Department of Transportation. My superiors assured me that if I would return to my ancestral roots of Buddhism, all charges would be dropped; otherwise, I would be terminated. I had one week to make a decision.

There was no decision to be made. I resigned my position that day and walked home, praying every step of the way. At home, I was surprised to find Lei, my mother, and two women from church on their knees in the living room. As I walked through the door, I heard my mother praying, "Jesus, I, too, trust you. I know that you are God and I deny Buddha and all of his teachings." I fell to my knees and joined in on the time of praise. God had just saved my mother.

The next two weeks were filled with joy and sadness. There was abundant joy that my mother had become a follower of Jesus and could not get enough of His teachings. She read the Bible for hours every day. There was sadness that I had no job, and my father and his friends continually harassed my family day and night. After six months of diligently searching for a job, I was hired at the Hotel Lisboa. It was not the job I wanted, but it put food on the table and paid my bills. I was very thankful.

Hotel Lisboa has nearly a thousand rooms and hosts the most famous casino in Macau. When I was hired, it was my understanding that I would work in the restaurant. However, I was placed in the casino. Since I needed the money, I kept the job even though I questioned whether I was out of God's will for working in such a place. I continued working in the casino every night and looking for a different occupation every day. Over time, I came to realize that it was God who had placed me in the casino. I shared the claims of Jesus with some sixty or so people, eleven of whom surrendered their own lives to the Lord. God had given me a new ministry.

Because most Christians looked down on anyone in the casino industry, the casino workers and showgirls who became believers did not feel comfortable around church people. Understanding their need for discipleship, I changed to the day shift and began a Bible study three nights a week in my home. My mother mentored the showgirls, Lei discipled the barmaids, and I guided the waiters, porters, and dealers. This worked well until my home became too small to hold everyone coming to study God's Word. I begged my pastor to let me use the church, but he was afraid of the reaction from the church members, so my plea was denied.

I rented a small warehouse just off the waterfront and began teaching Bible studies there. I never asked anyone for money, yet somehow people began to give me money to help pay for the building and expenses. By the end of the year, we were holding Bible studies five nights a week. I became so exhausted from working six days a week and teaching five nights a week that my body crashed. I was in bed for three days with a high fever.

I knew I could not continue working and teaching, so I decided to trust Jesus with my finances. I gave my resignation to the hotel management so I could study and teach God's Word. He has more than provided for my needs. He has abundantly poured out His blessings on Lei and me. Counting the two Sunday morning Bible studies, we now offer Bible studies to eleven different groups every week. Seeing the great need, we expanded our ministry to include ex-prostitutes. Lei has led more than two dozen prostitutes to faith in Christ, and every Monday night my mother disciples them.

I realize that I am not called to be a pastor, but I am called to be a lay leader who can make an eternal difference in Macau. I am simply a student and teacher of the Word of God. I have no idea why people are drawn to my Bible studies, because I am not eloquent nor am I a scholar. I guess the Lord is just drawing men and women to Himself and He found a few vessels that He could use here in Macau.

My only regret in life is that my father died without ever trusting Jesus as his Savior. Indeed, he harassed us until the day he died, but in the end, God received glory even from my father's death. When my father died, he left behind eight thousand dollars in the bank, money my mother did not want for herself. She asked me to "do something good with it."

So I rented a billboard for six months that read, "I wasted my life and missed my opportunity to spend eternity with Jesus. Don't miss your chance. Accept Jesus *now,* or you, too, will meet my tragic fate." It was signed, "A Victim in Hell."

Such an action may come across as harsh and unfeeling, but it is neither. I loved my father, and I know Jesus loved my father. Nevertheless, my father despised the name of Jesus and rejected Him on every occasion. For most of his life my father thought nothing of spending eternity separated from the Lord, though now I am sure he does. And I do not want any more fathers, or anyone for that matter, taking the road that leads to destruction. Like the rich man who begged God to send someone to his family, my father may be begging the same. If so, I may be fulfilling my father's wishes. God's Word is the avenue that leads to repentance and salvation, an avenue I pray will be filled with the thousands in Macau who desperately need Him.

— PART FOUR —

SECULARIST/COMMUNIST PERSECUTION

CHAPTER FIFTEEN

A Brilliant Light to My People
The Story of Fai
(China)

*Now to Him who is able to do exceedingly abundantly
above all that we ask or think, according to the power that
works in us, to Him be glory in the church by Christ Jesus
throughout all ages, world without end. Amen.*
—EPHESIANS 3:20–21

I was nine years old when I watched my father face death. In a seemingly routine visit to the doctor, my father unexpectedly learned that he would die within two months. With each day, I watched him become more terrified of his impending death.

I hurt for him as I looked into my father's eyes because I could see him being consumed by fear. His body, which had seemed healthy just days earlier, suddenly was wrenched with physical pain and emotional agony. His eyes darted back and forth, as though he was trying to grasp every second of life. This was the first time I had witnessed such fear. It was so intense that I wanted to escape, but he wanted to continually tell me stories about his life, so I could not leave him alone. He was making sure I never forgot him. He was without faith and without hope.

As a young boy growing up on the outskirts of Beijing, I occasionally went to the temple with my mother's parents. They were Buddhists and appeared to be somewhat committed to their faith. Yet, my father held his Buddhist tradition in tension with a staunch atheism. He submitted to the Communist Party doctrines. I remember that he mocked my grandparents for their faith in Buddha and cursed Christians who lived near our home. He had no room in his life for God.

On the day of his death, my father did not speak in coherent sentences most of the day. However, when I suggested that he might find relief from his fear in religion, he became infuriated and screamed, "Fai, if you ever mention religion in this house again, you can eat and sleep on the streets with the rest of the dogs. I will not tolerate such foolishness!" Less than an hour later he died. These last, piercing words burned into my mind.

His deathbed statement stunned me. All I wanted to do was bring a little relief and hope to a miserable, dying man. I thought of my grandparent's faith in Buddhism, a faith that seemed to bring peace to them. I also pondered the faith of a friend named Travis, an American who was a follower of Jesus. Surely one of these religions would have helped ease my father's pain and calm his fears. I just knew that if my father could have believed in some sort of god, he would have had more peace.

After Father's death, my mother and I moved in with my grandparents. Their home was small, so Mother and I shared a room. She slept on an old, makeshift bed, and I had a pallet on the floor. The pallet consisted of two thin blankets and a well-worn pillow. Since my grandparents lived on the opposite side of Beijing, I never saw my friend Travis again. I have thought of him over the years, and often wonder what became of him. As a child I wanted to visit Travis because I was intrigued by his faith in Jesus.

My mother and I were forced to attend the Buddhist temple with my grandparents until I was seventeen. I would try to appease Buddha by lighting incense at his altar. I presented him with lotus flowers and rubbed gold on his statues. I prayed at least once a week, but none of these rituals made any difference. I knew that Buddhism was empty, so I stopped visiting the temples as soon as I was out of the home.

At seventeen, I went to college. I studied Western business and learned

English over the four-year course. During my third year of studies, my college employed an American teacher. Philip was an excellent communicator who understood Chinese culture, so he could explain Western ideas and show their practical applications in a Chinese business context.

In early November of that third year, my mother became extremely ill. I received word to come home, as she was near death. I stayed home for ten days, and by then my mother was much improved. Her doctor was amazed. So I confidently returned to school. Upon my return, Philip inquired of my mother and told me that he had been praying for her. Out of curiosity I asked why he had prayed for her. Philip explained to me how his own mother had been deathly sick some years earlier. Several people had asked Jesus to heal her, and his mother's health had improved. I thanked him for his prayer and returned to class.

Over the next five months, Philip and I had tea at the campus teahouse several times a month. One evening as I arrived at the restaurant, I noticed Philip was sitting at a table in the corner. I could tell by his face that he was deeply troubled. That night Philip opened up his heart to me. "Fai, I need to tell you a story that changed my life," he began. During the evening, Philip explained how Jesus had made an impact on his life. He told of struggles with depression and alcoholism. He related that when no one else would love him, Jesus reached down from heaven and loved him. It was a gripping tale of how Jesus died on a cross in order to save people. By the end of his story we were both in tears.

Suddenly, Philip looked at me and said, "Fai, Jesus died for you too. Have you ever considered trusting Jesus with your life?" My knees were shaking so badly that the tablecloth was swaying side to side. Not knowing how to respond, I blurted out, "Philip, I'm an atheist. I cannot trust in Jesus." My experience with Buddhism had taught me that religion was hopeless and empty. Atheism had sounded good to me at the time. Over the next hour we discussed the importance of trusting in the right things.

After dinner, Philip and I walked back to the campus together. As I was about to enter the dorm, Philip handed a book to me. "Fai, read this," he said as he turned and proceeded down the steps. There was not enough light by the doorway to read the book's title, so I tucked it under my right arm and went to my room. I entered my room and tossed the book on my bed. Then I noticed that it was a Bible. I quickly threw my jacket over it. I had three roommates, and I was fearful of how they would react to a Bible in the room. Later I hid the Bible between my mattresses.

Three months later, Philip returned to America. I was sad to see him go. He was an excellent instructor, and I knew that he cared for his students. I always wondered if he had spoken privately with other students about Jesus, but no one ever mentioned it.

Two years later, I graduated from the college and began working as a translator for local government officials in Changsha, in southern China. The weather is much milder than that of Beijing. I enjoyed living in a new city that was beautiful, with lush trees and flowers much of the year. However, I quickly became disillusioned with my government position.

My job required me to translate documents from English into Chinese and explain the meaning, context, and nuances of the documents to my employers. I tried to explain what I knew of Western ideals and thought. I quickly found out that Western business culture had a higher ethical standard than that of the people in my office. I was regularly instructed to alter documents so it would look as if the officials had done better financially than they had. I knew what I was doing was wrong, but I did it anyway. I had a premier job. Everyone seemed to want to be my friend.

Nine months after moving to Changsha, while unpacking one of my last boxes, I found the Bible that Philip had given to me. I had never opened it. That night, sitting on the floor in my living room, I opened the Bible and was surprised to find a note written to me inside the front cover. "Fai, may this copy of God's Word bring you peace and joy in this life and bring you eternal life with Jesus in the next life (John 3:16)." It was signed, "Your friend forever, Philip." For the first time since I had become an adult, tears streamed down my face. They dropped onto the pages of the book. I had not thought of Philip in over a year, but now memories came flooding back.

I turned to the Gospel of John. It took me several minutes to find it. After reading John 3:16, I decided to read the entire book of John. Over the next five nights, I read the entire book. It was interesting but nothing significant happened. After completing the book, I placed the Bible on a shelf in my bedroom, where it sat collecting dust for another year.

After working in Changsha for nearly two years, I met Graham, a British businessman who wanted to export handcrafts from Changsha to England. He came to Changsha to negotiate with the proper officials, my superiors. Graham and I worked together for five long, exhausting days, translating and negotiating this agreement.

On the following Saturday night, I stopped by a coffee house on my way home and saw Graham sitting in the corner, drinking coffee and reading a book. He invited me to sit with him. I inquired into his reading and learned that he was reading a Bible—in public. I became somewhat nervous, as I did not want to be associated with the Bible. Chinese politics and religion do not mix well. The Red Party denies all religions, but they especially hate Christianity. The Communist Party seems to fear the Christians more because Christians have an attitude of freedom, even when bound by prison. It was in my best interest to be an atheist.

I was about to excuse myself politely when Graham said, "Tell me, Fai, have you ever seen or read the Bible before?" Sheepishly, I replied that I had read the book of John. Then we launched into a three-hour conversation. Graham explained things to me in a way I never before understood. He also told me his own story of how Jesus changed his life through the Gospel of John. By the time I left the café, I had promised to read John again.

When the next morning arrived I felt restless. I took my Bible, which was hidden in a brown paper bag, and headed toward the park. I sat down by the lake and spent the entire day reading the book of John. I read the fourteenth chapter several times. All night long I pondered that part of John. It was a difficult night. I was keenly aware that something in my life was wrong, but I had no idea what. I tossed and turned and got out of bed and went outside to sit. Thoughts raced through my mind concerning this Jesus that John seemed to know so well. Even though I was resistant, deep down I desired to know Him also.

Monday morning, I arrived at the office an hour early to finish the paperwork that would conclude our business with Graham. Once all the papers were signed Graham would be back on a plane for London and out of my life forever—or so I thought. The final series of meetings lasted until 7:30 PM. Graham then asked me to accompany him to dinner to cover some last-minute changes that needed to be made. I felt obligated and agreed.

That night I told Graham of my sleepless night. After dinner, I walked with Graham back to his hotel. As we walked, I remembered Travis and his father reading the Bible. I could almost see Philip's face as I recalled my conversations with him. The walk to the hotel was a time of rapid reflection.

Graham and I sat in the lobby discussing John 14:1–6 until 11:30. I came to understand that Jesus truly was the Son of God. Just before midnight, I went up to Graham's room, held his Bible next to my chest, and with quivering lips declared Jesus Christ as my Savior. What a relief came over me. I was free at last. All fear and anxiety were gone. Nothing was left inside of me except peace and contentment.

The first month after my salvation was exhilarating. I began reading the New Testament every night. My outlook on life was incredibly optimistic, and I began witnessing to my coworkers. That is when the problems started. My supervisor heard that I had become a Christian, and he called me into his office. He said, "I want to remind you that you signed an oath to be an atheist before you were hired. Now I hear that you are a Christian. Is that true?" he began. Fearing for my job, I replied, "No, sir, there is no god! Never has been. Never will be!" I personally understood the pressure that the apostle Peter must have felt when he too denied Jesus.

That night, as I entered my bedroom, my Bible seemed to stare back at me. It was as though it knew that I had betrayed it. I continued to read my Bible every night, but I kept silent at the office. Four months passed, and with each passing month, my feelings of guilt intensified. By my sixth month of salvation, my soul was so torn within that I approached my supervisor and told him the truth. With trembling hands and shaking knees, I quiveringly uttered, "Mr. Wang, please forgive me for lying to you. I am a Christian. I believe that Jesus Christ is the Son of God. I can deny Him no longer."

I was fired immediately. Later that week I was evicted from my apartment. My landlord was instructed to get rid of me as soon as possible or he would face official reprimand. I was locked out of my apartment and not allowed even to collect my clothes. As I walked down the steps, my Bible sailed by my head and hit the floor in front of me. I tucked it under my arm and left the building. Later, I was held in jail for three days and nights for "being a troublemaker." As soon as I was released from jail, I went to the bank and closed my account. I walked out with my life savings of six hundred thirty dollars and took a train to Beijing in hopes of a new start.

Unfortunately, word reached Beijing before I did. I lived in Beijing for seven months, applied for nearly fifty positions, and was turned down at the beginning of each interview. "Fai, you are more than qualified, but we do not hire troublemakers. Our records indicate that you are a Christian. Are our records incorrect?" I would hear it over and over again. Every time I replied, "No, your records are correct." Every time they responded by telling me that I was not suitable for their company. The Communist Party has a long reach into the business sector.

I continued reading my Bible. I was reading Ephesians 3:20–21 when God intervened. As I was entering a supermarket I met Pichet, a longtime friend from college. He was working with a software company and told me of a position that was available. I told him of my problems, but he did not seem to think that it would be an issue. He gave me an address and told me to see Mr. Wong. The next day I went to see Mr. Wong, and he hired me immediately, without even looking at my résumé. Pichet had a keen business sense and had saved the company four hundred thousand dollars in two years. He had been promoted and was Mr. Wong's boss, and Pichet had instructed Mr. Wong to hire me.

I worked for the software company five years before I learned that Pichet was a Christian as well. My old friend, Philip, had shared Christ with Pichet, too, and led him to faith in Jesus Christ. Pichet himself had been witnessing to people for years and had started seventeen house churches. He had personally led over two hundred people to faith in Christ. Pichet and I began teaching Bible studies together.

I enjoyed five years of personal instruction from Pichet as God used him to teach me to trust Jesus in every situation of life. However, none of his Bible studies, lectures, or his sermons taught me more than did watching my friend approach his coming death. When Pichet went to be with Jesus in 1996, his body has been destroyed by cancer. However, his spirit was strong and vibrant. I was at his bedside with his wife and son. His son was holding one hand while I held the other. Pichet smiled and said, "I will see all of you later. I will be waiting with Jesus for your arrival." What a striking contrast to the fear that attended my father's death.

After ten years with the software company, I resigned. I sensed a call to preach the gospel of Jesus Christ. Six of the house churches that Pichet had started and three that I had begun met together. After their meeting, they asked me to become their regional pastor. I agreed, and today I am a bivocational church planter. I freelance myself out to troubleshoot software when I need money, but my real passion is sharing Jesus. I have been planting churches since I left the security of my job, and I have not lacked anything. God has supplied from His riches in glory. He has allowed me to be a part of two hundred church plants throughout China.

Though I have baptized more than three hundred persons, my greatest joy came when I led my own mother to Christ and baptized her. I had given her a Bible. After more than two years of questions, she surrendered her heart to Jesus in April 2004. At age sixty-eight, she was so frail that she had to be carried into the river to be baptized. Even so, her faith was strong that day. I, as her son, was allowed to take part in this illustration of the power of Christ to give new life to anyone who believes. Suddenly I was struck by the fact that my mother had named me Fai, which means "a brilliant light."

From time to time, I am still harassed by the local and provincial authorities for preaching in house churches. Police have forced several of our churches to disband. Afterward they always restart, with more passion and vigor than before. Occasionally the police will detain me for five or ten days without filing any charges. Yet, in the midst of perpetual persecution, God works mightily. The last time I was jailed, I shared the good news with several people, and a police guard gave his heart to Christ. My prayer is that, wherever I am, I may walk with the Lord in such a way that brings light to my people.

CHAPTER SIXTEEN

IN THE MIDST OF FREEDOM
The Story of Nicolai
(Russia)

And above all things have fervent love for one another, for
"love will cover a multitude of sins."
—1 PETER 4:8

In late 1989, the world watched as the Berlin Wall was finally torn down. Freedom was unstoppable in the satellite states of the former Soviet Union. Millions of people were set free from the tyranny of a Communist system that had been set in place nearly seventy-five years earlier. Most assumed that freedom had come to all Eastern Europeans. But that was not the case.

I grew up under the heavy hand of Soviet Communist Party dictators. I worked for some of them, including Nikita Khrushchev, Leonid Brezhnev, and Mikhail Gorbachev. I was willing to do anything needed to protect Mother Russia from her enemies. But little did I know that I would need protection from her one day.

Ironically, the persecution I encountered did not begin until after the Soviet government had collapsed. While millions of Russians were experiencing freedom for the first time in their lives, the old power system was still functioning and was persecuting some of us for our "crimes against the homeland." They still held out hope that the old system would not be entirely dismantled, and they were trying desperately to hold on to power where they could. I was pressed under the weight of religious persecution in the early 1990s. I was imprisoned for four years for nothing more than being a Christian in Russia. While many Russians tasted freedom gleefully and immediately, I would have to wait to see the result of freedom.

My life is a reminder that freedom intended for all does not always come to all. Furthermore, religious liberty, when enacted into law, takes time to enforce. Of all freedoms, religious freedom is the most important freedom and perhaps the most difficult to attain.

At the age of nineteen, I was recruited as an undercover policeman, a job I held for the next thirty-two years. Most of those years were spent in the lobby of Hotel Ukraina, where my assignment was to gather information on Soviet and Western politicians and businessmen by building relationships with them. I posed as a wealthy businessman hungry for power and wealth. Normally I could acquire enough information on an individual to have them arrested within two hours.

I am not proud that I played a part in the arrests of about twelve hundred people during my thirty-two years of service. It was my job. I did it for my country, or so I was told. Most of the people I had arrested were taken in for petty violations. However, most were found guilty of treason in the end.

I was sitting in the hotel restaurant one bone-chilling December night. Outside, the Moskva River was nearly frozen solid, the wind was howling, and snow was falling so hard that every time the front door was opened, snow would blow in up to the reception desk. As always, I was in the restaurant near the doorway when a Russian man named Miroslav sat down at the table next to me. He and his wife shared a meal together for what seemed to them to be a wonderfully pleasant evening. As soon as they retired to their room, I called my superior and had the man arrested. Miroslav had broken one of Russia's Cardinal Laws. He had made a reference to Jesus Christ. Since Miroslav worked for the city of Moscow in the upper levels of the finance ministry, I was obligated to turn him in for violating his governmental covenant to be an avowed atheist. I heard Miroslav declare that Jesus Christ is God. He told his wife that they must be very careful to keep their faith a secret. Little did they know who I was or what I had heard.

Miroslav was fired and imprisoned for two years. The official charge was related to mishandling of government funds, which, of course, was not true. The reason for his punishment was his refusal to deny Jesus. Miroslav and his wife lost everything. She was forced to move in with her parents until Miroslav was released from prison. After his release, he could not find a good job because every employer was afraid of the secret police. I never meant to inflict such pain on people like Miroslav. I only wanted to protect Mother Russia.

My assignment with the secret police inflicted pain on so many people that it became difficult to sleep at night. Some of those arrested were truly criminals and needed to be put behind bars or sent off to Siberia. However, too many of them were imprisoned, or worse, for nothing more than being Christian. Mother Russia did not seem to care if the general populous was religious, but the powerful and influential were required to remain atheists.

I could not have imagined that I, too, would one day fall to the same laws by which Miroslav had been arrested. The persecutor became the persecuted. One bitterly cold night, just after my forty-eighth birthday, I was working at Hotel Ukraina. Walking down the front steps of the hotel, I fell on the slippery ice and snow. Suddenly a man named Ilya extended a hand to me and helped me to my feet. He escorted me back into the restaurant, as I could barely walk because my right foot was fractured. Ilya and I shared a pot of tea and talked for close to three hours.

It became clear during the conversation that Ilya had a different demeanor from that of most Russians. This retired Soviet commander was not cold, indifferent, and downright callous, as were the other commanders I had known so well. He was genuinely concerned for my well-being. He even offered to take me to his physician to have the foot examined. It was this genuine concern for me that made me want to know him better.

During the six months that followed my fall, Ilya and I met six or seven times for dinner and became close friends. One night I was at his flat having dinner when I noticed a Bible on his bookshelf. When I inquired about the book, he told me that he was a Christian: "Nicolai, I have found peace for my soul in that book. The demons that used to haunt me have been put to rest because of what Jesus has done in my life." Ilya began to tell horror stories of atrocities that he had been forced to inflict on people while a military commander.

"I have killed so many that only Jesus could silence the voices of the innocent," he said.

Ilya described how he had become a follower of the teachings of Jesus, and how he was forced to retire from military service. He was even forced to sign a document of loyalty that contained a testament of his commitment to atheism. "I wish I had never signed it, but I feared for my own life as well as the life of my wife," Ilya explained.

Ilya took the Bible from the shelf and read from the Gospel of John. It was filled with stories of Jesus and His love. "Nicolai, Jesus can bring peace to you, too, if you will only trust Him," Ilya pleaded.

"Thank you for dinner, but I must go now," I hastily replied. I walked down the steps to the street below, trying to hold back my tears. I wondered how Ilya knew that I needed peace for my soul. Was it written on my forehead? I cried as I made my way to the bus stop and slept very little that night. In fact, I slept very little for the next week. All I could think of was that I indeed needed peace.

A month later, Ilya was back in the Hotel Ukraina having lunch with one of Moscow's city officials. I entered the dining room through the kitchen so I would not be noticed by Ilya. Quietly, I sat directly behind him. Mostly, he was talking about superficial family matters, but there was one point that I heard him say, "Just stop by my home on Sunday evening. There will be several believers there. Come join us."

Now I was faced with the dilemma of my life. Was I going to report Ilya concerning what I had just heard? Immediately, I exited through the kitchen and tried to sort it out in my mind. What was I to do? I thought on this issue for over a month, but I just could not bring myself to report him. I decided that I needed to speak with Ilya. I made an appointment to meet with him at his home and paid him a visit.

I explained to him that I had overheard the conversation with the Moscow official. Surprisingly, he did not seem overly concerned. Instead, he encouraged me to "do what you honestly believe is the right thing to do." He treated me with such kindness that I found myself admiring him. How could this man be a threat to Mother Russia? I did not tell Ilya, but that night I decided that I would never turn him in to the authorities. Keeping my mouth shut was the right thing to do. As I was leaving Ilya's home that night, he invited me to join him and some friends to study the Bible the following Sunday night. I just looked at him without a reply as I left the flat.

Sunday night I was at his Bible study along with eight other people. One of those present was the city official who was a believer in Jesus. In fact, he opened the meeting by praying to Jesus. Three hours later, after everyone else had gone home, Ilya asked me, "Nicolai, why do you find it so difficult to believe that Jesus is God?" We talked until two o'clock in the morning. As I put on my coat to leave, Ilya handed me a Bible and asked me to read the New Testament.

Periodically, I attended the Bible studies at Ilya's home over the next two years. Finally, one Sunday evening, not long after my fiftieth birthday, I asked Jesus to be my Lord and Savior. I remember that night as though it were today. When I asked Jesus to forgive me for all of my sins, I remember the feeling of freedom that came upon me for the first time in my life. It was a wonderful night. I had been set free by the truth.

The year following my conversion was a time of joy and pain. I grew in the joy of my salvation, but I grew increasingly weary in my job. For two consecutive months I gave no new information at all to my superiors, so arrests were drastically reduced. Little did I realize that I had become suspect. The secret police assigned two men to monitor me. Shortly after I turned fifty-three years old, I was arrested and charged with conspiring against Mother Russia. I was labeled a spy and sentenced to life in prison. No evidence was presented against me, only accusations that I, an official agent of Mother Russia, had consorted with known conspirators and was, therefore, a traitor.

I was detained for nine months before I was given an opportunity to defend myself. At my hearing, I was asked only one question: "Are you a Christian or a Russian?" My heart stopped. What was I to say? I responded, "Yes, I follow the teachings of Jesus Christ. He is the God of my soul. But let it be known that I am also a Russian. I am a Russian who loves Jesus."

I spent the next four years in prison. The first year I was in solitary confinement, in contact only with the guards who fed me. Finally I was allowed to enter the general population. The three-year imprisonment that followed was not as terrible as I anticipated. Russian prisons do not normally allow visitors, but Ilya was granted permission to visit one time. Knowing exactly what I needed, Ilya slipped in a New Testament through his military connections. That Bible helped me keep my sanity. I was a forced laborer for fifteen hours a day, but at night I read my Bible. One night, one of my three cellmates, who was illiterate, asked me to read the Bible to him. Starting at the very first chapter of the New Testament, I began reading from five to ten chapters a night.

By the time I finished the apostle Paul's letter to the Ephesians, I had led two of my three cellmates to faith in Christ. The three of us shared our faith with others during the workday. We wanted to lead others to Christ, but quickly realized that we needed to spend non-work time with the other inmates to get an effective hearing. So we devised a plan.

Lesta, one of my cellmates, and I pretended to fight one evening. We even threw a couple of blows to convince the guards. Then we demanded to be placed in separate cells. The guards put us in solitary confinement for three weeks, but then we were transferred to the general population and reassigned to new cells. The plan worked better than expected. Three cells were having Bible readings at night. That meant I had to divide my Bible into three portions. I gave Lesta the four Gospels, I took Acts to Ephesians, and I gave Philippians to Revelation to Boris (the other convert in the cell).

Five of our nine new cellmates became believers. Now twelve followers of Jesus were in the prison. The plan worked flawlessly until one of our cellmates sold us out.

One night two guards escorted me from my cell and told me that they knew that I was the ringleader of a conspiracy to overthrow Mother Russia. I assured them that I had no desire nor plan to do anything of the sort. "You Christians always lie. You must pay for your treachery, Christian," one of the guards muttered as he began hitting me with his baton. Soon both men were furiously hitting me with batons. It seemed to last for hours, but in reality it took about ten minutes for me to lose consciousness.

I came to back in my cell. The guards informed my cellmates that I had fallen down the steps and that I should be more careful. I was never taken to see the doctor. But, then, I never saw a doctor during the time I was in prison. I believed this persecution would never end, yet a few months later, after four years, I suddenly was released. I still am not sure how my freedom was secured, but Ilya met me as I was dismissed from the prison bus, just outside Moscow. During the years I was imprisoned, Ilya had started nine house churches. These small fellowships immediately showed their generosity by taking up a collection to help me settle into a small flat. Ilya himself helped me find a job selling Christmas ornaments at a mall near Red Square. I worked days in the mall and attended Bible studies three nights a week.

By spring, a Bible study of fifteen met in my home every Thursday night. Shortly thereafter, I sensed that the Lord wanted me to split the group into three groups of five so we could have three separate Bible studies. God was leading me personally to shepherd the believers. The others did as well, so we began treating our fellowship as a church. Soon all of the Bible studies grew into churches, and by November, I was shepherding five house churches and discipling eleven pastors.

Eight months later I had my first heart attack. I had been working four days a week selling Christmas ornaments, and two days a week taking tourists through Basil's Cathedral in Red Square. I preached and taught in house churches five nights a week, and discipled shepherds two nights a week. It was my heart's deepest desire to see Russia worship Christ, and I wanted to do my part. But my heart attack showed that God wanted me to slow down. So, I quit my job at Basil's Cathedral and combined my shepherding to one night. Even with a reduced work schedule, two years later I had a second heart attack.

I was sixty-four years old, and once again I needed to reduce my workload. I had led some two hundred people to faith in Jesus Christ, planted thirty-five house churches, and discipled nearly seventy shepherds. Life had taken its toll on my body, and I physically could not keep pace with the vision that God had given to me. I decided to shepherd one church and agreed to disciple other pastors only two nights a week.

I still sell Christmas ornaments four days a week, but now work only half days.

My physical ailments have forced me to set priorities for the latter part of my life. I have two prayers. I pray that the Lord will continue to give me health and opportunity to serve Him until He takes me home. I also ask that God will allow me to encounter some of those I have wronged so that I may be reconciled with them and share how Jesus has made such a difference in my life. The Lord forgave me long ago. I also would like to seek their forgiveness. Whether that happens, I still am amazed how Jesus Christ could forgive a sinner such as I.

CHAPTER SEVENTEEN

A Reminder of Past Sacrifices
The Story of Hao
(Vietnam)

*We are confident, yes, well pleased rather to be absent from
the body and to be present with the Lord.*
—2 Corinthians 5:8

When American troops pulled out of South Vietnam in 1975, there was a sense of relief, or at least resignation, in the United States. They were glad that young American men were removed from the dangers of battle, yet many soldiers returned home without anyone showing them gratitude for their risk and sacrifice. Within a few months, the Viet Cong had taken control and set up a communist dictatorship. Many Vietnamese who had opposed the communists faced retribution.

Many in the United States believed that the war was hopeless and meaningless, so it was better to cut their losses. Yet, those soldiers were not merely protecting American security; they were protecting Vietnamese freedom. After the withdrawal, the Vietnamese had no hope of freedom.

Today, Vietnam officials argue that the state allows religious freedom, but that claim is false. Nearly every Vietnamese evangelical encounters problems with authorities. Recently, four Mennonites I know were imprisoned and charged with resisting police officers after a scuffle broke out. An undercover policeman was monitoring the Mennonite church in Ho Chi Minh City (formerly Saigon). One day the police attempted to force Mennonites in Kontum and Gia Lai provinces to sign declarations renouncing their religion.

Even the "legal Catholics" are having problems. At least three Roman Catholics are serving long prison sentences for teaching Bible courses. Others are imprisoned for distributing religious books. Sixty-four-year-old Father Pham Minh Tri has been imprisoned at Z30A prison in Dong Nai for eighteen years and has suffered from dementia for most of the past ten years. Although my homeland is long since forgotten by most Americans, its fate is a reminder of communism's hostility toward religion.

I heard stories of persecution before I became a follower of Jesus, but I was a twenty-year-old atheist. Religious persecution was not directed at me personally. Then one day my heart and perspective changed. I met a man who told me about the Lord, Jesus Christ. Then the persecution became very real and personal. Once I decided to live by the teachings of Jesus, I quickly realized the need for religious freedom.

My father's conversion to Christ, years before my own, first illustrated the love of Christ to me. One evening my father came home from work rejoicing that Jesus had changed his life. He shared how a friend from work had been talking with him about Jesus Christ for months. That day at work, my father asked Jesus to forgive his sins, and he began to follow the teachings of Jesus. I did not understand exactly what that meant, but I quickly noticed changes in my father's attitude and behavior.

Before my father became a follower of Jesus, he drank excessive amounts of alcohol and verbally abused my mother and me every day. However, from the day of his conversion, my father never drank alcohol, nor did he use profanity. My father displayed a new character and compassion that I could never have imagined.

The next month, our family began attending a little church near our home, about an hour from downtown Ho Chi Minh City. It was a small church that met in an old storefront building next door to a seafood restaurant. My father, understanding his role as the leader of the family, required that my mother, two sisters, and I attend church every Sunday. Even though I was twenty and a student in college, I was expected to be in church regularly. I never paid much attention to what was taking place, but I did not mind going. After worship, my father would almost always take us to lunch at the seafood restaurant.

That summer, my father was killed when a tractor-trailer truck ran a traffic signal and hit his motorcycle. Suddenly I was the family's primary means of support. I dropped out of college and began working as a waiter in Highlands Coffee Shop. It was difficult supporting my family on my salary of eighty dollars a month, but somehow we survived.

Most of the people that I met at Highlands Coffee were tourists, since only elite Vietnamese could afford the restaurant prices. One evening in late October, I waited on Tom and his wife Yvette, Americans working as translators for American corporations. Tom and Yvette became regulars. I would see them at least three times a week.

At first, Tom seemed a little strange. He would bring a Bible with him to read as he sipped his cup of deep, black, Vietnamese-blend coffee. One morning, there were not very many people in the café so Tom asked me to sit with him for a moment. He began asking me questions about the culture. So I described to him how twenty-first-century Vietnamese view life. Then he asked about my life. I shared what it was like to be a young Vietnamese man. He seemed interested in me and my problems. Tom said that he would pray that God would help me work things out for my family. That very day, I got a promotion to assistant manager. My salary increased to one hundred and ten dollars a month. That got my attention, and I wanted to know more about Tom and his God.

Right on schedule, Tom came for coffee two mornings later. I immediately told him of my promotion, but he did not appear to be surprised. It was as though he expected it. He said, "Hao, God has answered my prayer because He loves you. He wants you to know Him just as I do."

Memories of my father came flooding back to me. I began to weep and told Tom about my father's decision to follow Jesus. I shared how Father had radically changed, so that I knew what he experienced was real. I added that I was rebelliously refusing to accept Jesus as my Lord. Then I asked, "How can God love me after I have told Him that I do not want Him? I rejected God even after I had watched Him change my father."

Tom took a Bible out of his backpack and opened it up to the Gospel of John. As he read John 15:9–17, I began to understand that the feeling I had been so desperately trying to resist was Jesus calling me unto Himself.

"If Jesus still wants me, I will follow His teachings for the rest of my life," I muttered through the sobbing. Right there on the fourth floor in the Highlands Coffee Shop, I bowed my knee and asked Jesus to forgive my rebelliousness, and asked Him to be my Savior and Lord. That November day changed my life forever.

I began attending church with Tom and Yvette, soaking up every sermon by the preacher. I met with Tom every Sunday night to study the Bible. He would teach me about Jesus, and Yvette would treat me to American sweets like chocolate cake, coconut cake, and brownies. During the years that followed, I grew spiritually.

One of Tom's neighbors notified the police that the American was up to something with a young Vietnamese man. The police placed listening devices in Tom's flat, taped our Bible studies, and wondered what we were doing when they heard us pray together. The government got rid of Tom and Yvette by not allowing them to renew their visas. I was arrested and sentenced to attend reeducation seminars every Saturday for a year. Each session lasted from ten in the morning until eight that night.

I did as I was told for the first five months. But the police noticed that I had not stopped attending church on Sunday. They arrested me. One Sunday, four policemen barged through the doors of the church in downtown Ho Chi Minh City, handcuffed me, dragged me by my arms out into the street, and beat me for ten minutes. They arrested the pastor and seventeen other church members for proselytizing a Vietnamese.

I was taken to jail in district five and left in the cell for ten days. When I was finally released, I went to the hospital and found out that four bones were broken. Two had to be rebroken before they could be reset.

Upon release from the hospital, I returned to work, only to find that I had been fired. The official word was that, since I had missed two weeks of work, I was not dependable. However, one of my friends informed me that the police had visited the manager and demanded that I be fired.

I was rapidly becoming a liability to my mother and sisters, so I moved in with a friend who offered me a room. Trey helped me find a job at a new upscale coffee shop frequented by the wealthiest Vietnamese. The very first night, I waited on a popular singer. She was beautiful, classy, and dressed like a Hollywood movie star. She was also quite proud of her status. I don't think I have ever met anyone else so arrogant. Yet, meeting her was not a total loss. Her manager left a ten-dollar tip.

My new job paid well. I earned eighty dollars a month and earned perhaps an additional twenty dollars in tips. I was still attending reeducation classes, and the police watched me so closely that I never went back to church. I was afraid of what the authorities would do to the pastor if I were to attend a service. Nevertheless, I continued to grow in the Lord and praised Him for His goodness.

Shortly after I moved in with Trey, he, too, became a follower of Jesus. We studied the Bible at least three nights a week. Within the next twelve months, Trey and I had shared the Good News of Jesus with at least fifty of our friends and family. In March, I started a Bible study in my mother's home with my mother, two sisters, and six other friends. To my amazement, all of my family have become believers in Jesus. Trey began a Bible study in our flat with ten friends from work, eight of whom were believers.

In a few months, the police visited my mother's home and our apartment, on the very night that we were having Bible studies. Every one of us was arrested and incarcerated in district three. I was singled out as the conspirator.

All were released after three days except for me. Each person paid a twenty-dollar fine for participating in an illegal gathering. However, I remained in jail for another month. Finally, in early June, a high-ranking official came to my cell. His first words to me were both abrupt and revealing: "Hao, are you stupid, son? What will it take for you to stop this foolishness concerning Jesus? Your father was run down for the same foolishness. Do you desire the same fate?"

I was speechless. My father was murdered because he refused to deny Jesus? Yes, my father, who worked for the postal service, was targeted by his own supervisor, who paid a truck driver to intentionally run him down. Then I understood why the driver never faced any charges. He had been ordered to do it. Tears came to my eyes. The emotions were just too intense to hold back.

I desperately wanted to hate this man. I wanted to lash out and sentence him to eternal punishment and damnation, but Jesus would not allow me to speak evil.

"My father had no choice," I finally blurted out. "My father loved Jesus more than life because Jesus called my father to believe in Him. Jesus has called me too. I have no choice. The decision was made two thousand years ago on a cross. I do not take your threat lightly, but you must know that some day you, too, will stand before God and give an account of your life and deeds. I urge you to become a follower of Jesus before it is too late for you."

In outrage, the official drew the pistol and placed the tip of the barrel on my forehead, just above my left eyebrow. "How dare you speak to me in such a manner! Do you not know that I hold your life in my hands? I give you a choice. Recant or die. You have no other options."

I began to pray, "Lord, give me strength to endure the pain. Into your hands, I give my life."

That very moment, I heard the hammer drop on the pistol, but I was still alive. As I looked up at the man, he was grasping his chest, a look of horror on his face. He was turning red and was not breathing. When he hit the cell floor, the two guards ran in like little mice. They were bumping into walls and running into each other. I stayed in the cell for at least an hour, but no one came back. It was just me and this dead official, still grasping his chest.

I decided to make my way to the front of the cellblock to see where everyone was, and I found five policemen hiding behind a desk. "Go, please just go. Do not have the angel kill us too," they cried. I sat down beside the policemen and assured them that I was no threat to them. The two guards who had been in my cell said that "the moment the official pulled the pistol's trigger, an angel appeared and gently touched him on the chest." They swore under oath that I never touched the man. They were convinced that an angel had come to my rescue, and they were afraid to touch me.

I was released immediately. The city coroner stated that he could find no cause of death. "The man was in perfect health. He should be alive. He must have had some sort of muscle spasm because his face was so distorted. Whatever killed this man brought much pain with it," the official report stated.

I have no idea what happened. I just know that I trusted my life to Jesus and He preserved it for a reason. I do not know what the future holds, but I am still holding Bible studies. I have shared Jesus with over three hundred people of Ho Chi Minh City. I work in a department store six days a week, and teach the Bible four nights a week. I have seen eighty friends and relatives come to faith in Christ.

I had the opportunity to share Jesus with the wife of the city official who died in my cell. She became a believer the first time she heard the gospel. Soon I was teaching a Bible study in her home. Even as a widow, she has a great deal of influence in the political system and she is using it for the cause of Christ.

The relic of communism is alive and well in this bustling city; I await the day when freedom will come. I am confident that the sacrifice of my father will not go unheeded by God. I am sure that the sacrifice that the Americans and other nations made will also be answered by Him. In a land whose recent past is drenched with blood and oppression, I dream of the day freedom will ring and persecution will end. Until then, we Christians of Vietnam will stand boldly for the cause of Christ, for we are heirs to His kingdom and inheritors of His riches.

CHAPTER EIGHTEEN

Old Habits Die Hard
The Story of Oksana
(Ukraine)

For the word of God is living and powerful, and sharper than any two-edged sword, piercing even to the division of soul and spirit, and of joints and marrow, and is a discerner of the thoughts and intents of the heart.

—HEBREWS 4:12

My beloved Ukraine is rich in Christian tradition. Legend has it that the apostle Andrew preached here and opened the eyes of Ukrainians to the gospel. Nearly a millennium later, Orthodox Christianity was established as the official religion of the state. It remains the dominant religion.

But when Vladimir Lenin imposed his version of socialistic communism on the people after the Russian Revolution of 1917, he also inaugurated severe persecution to suppress the Orthodox Church, which he blamed for the troubles of the region. In time, his atheistic agenda included evangelicals in the crosshairs of the communist government. One of those persecuted was my maternal grandmother, a devout believer. When the Russians took control of Kiev, she was held at gunpoint and forced to confess that Jesus was a myth. She was one of millions brutalized by a succession of local and USSR Communist Party leaders. Thousands were imprisoned, exiled, beaten, and put to death. Churches were closed and overt Christianity nearly exterminated from many regions. My grandmother was an incredible and bold witness in my family lineage, yet my parents rejected Christian faith and adopted the worldview of those who persecuted my grandmother. They were atheists who believed that religion was mere foolishness in which one should not waste time. I grew up in Odessa, a Black Sea port city. My home was so close to this beautiful sea that I could view it from my rooftop. In fact, as a child, I climbed up on the roof at least once a week during the summer just to watch the ships go by. I loved living in Odessa, but we moved to Zhytomyr, Ukraine, when I was fourteen years old. My father left his position as a physician in the Odessa hospital and became chief of staff in Zhytomyr's hospital.

Among our new neighbors in Zhytomyr was a Christian family. Peter, the father, had two sons and a daughter who was the same age as me. Vera and I became best of friends. I knew she was a Christian, and she knew I was not, but it was not an issue between us. Even my parents seemed to accept my relationship to Vera for three years. While we knew many teenage girls who were out smoking, drinking, and living immorally, Vera and I were different. Vera taught me that I was special and that I should keep myself pure and free from tobacco, alcohol, and immorality. I knew those morals came out of her deeply held religious convictions, but they also seemed like the right way to live.

One weekend, my parents went to Kiev for special training. My sister spent the weekend with my aunt and I stayed with Vera's family. As I expected, the entire family went to church on Sunday morning. They did not force me to go, but they offered the opportunity, which I accepted. It was one of those days in Zhytomyr where it snows lightly all day. It was just cold enough that we needed to wear a coat.

As I walked through the doors of Central Baptist Church, I was astounded. It was not at all what I expected. There was an old, coal stove in the corner of the auditorium that provided only enough heat to barely knock the chill out of the air. I removed my coat and hung it among the others on a wooden coat rack by the back door. We sat on wooden benches with slats and sang songs for nearly an hour. Then the pastor walked up to this big desk, opened his Bible, and spoke on the evils of sinning, and shared how Jesus died to forgive us of all of our sins. For the first time in my life I heard I was a sinner.

Over the next four years, I went to church with Vera a dozen times or more. On one occasion, Vera asked me to go with her to hear a guest speaker from America named Edward. The American preached that morning on the desire of God to use Christians for His good and His glory. He spoke of how God, in His sovereignty, allows suffering in Christians' lives in order to mold them into His image so that they may serve Him even more. He insisted, "It all begins by trusting Jesus as your Lord and Savior." For the first time in my life, I felt like a sinner.

I knew that I had done wrong things, but I never felt like this. Something inside of me was wrong. I had to speak with this man. Vera and I waited for more than half an hour to speak to Edward. Many people wanted to talk to him, but finally it was our turn. I described to Edward how I felt inside and he assured me that what I was sensing was God drawing close to me. "Jesus died for you, Oksana. He loves you and wants you to know Him. All you have to do is trust Him," he said.

I knew Edward was right. I needed to trust Jesus with my life, so I prayed and asked Jesus to forgive me of my sin and I committed my life to Him. That day when I left Central Baptist Church, I was a changed person. My heart was pure and I knew it.

Vera and her family rejoiced with me. However, I was afraid to tell my parents because I knew they were strongly devoted to atheism. Thus, I waited for nearly a year before I even approached them on the matter. I had been baptized and had been a member of Central Baptist for six months before my parents knew of my conversion.

They found out, but not because of any boldness on my part. Rather, my mother found out by contact with a church member. My mother was making her rounds at the hospital visiting her patients when she met Valya. My mother introduced herself, and Valya replied, "Oh, you must be Oksana's mother." My mother chatted with her for a moment and said that, yes, I was her daughter. "We are so happy to have Oksana in our church," said Valya. "She is such a godly young woman. She is a joy to be around."

That evening, when I returned home from school, I had some explaining to do. My mother was angrier with me for not telling her of my decision than she was over my conversion itself. My father, however, was a different story. He lectured me for hours on the foolishness of religion. He did not forbid me from attending church, but he let me know in no uncertain terms how disappointed he was in me.

I continued attending Central Baptist Church until I graduated from the university with a teaching degree. I was given a position in Kiev. I had grown spiritually over the years, but I was not prepared to step into the atheists' world as a teacher. My first three months in Kiev were great, until my superior, Aleksander, found out I was a Christian. I was fired from my teaching post. When I inquired as to the reason I was fired, I was told, "You Christians are too unstable to teach. I do not want you infecting the minds of gullible young people."

My father had friends at the hospital in Kiev who arranged for me to teach at a private school. As it turns out, the school was a Christian school for the children of expatriates. Teaching in the school was wonderful. All of the teachers were Christians and we all had such good fellowship. I moved in and shared a flat with Hana, a teacher from Western Europe. Hana was a great roommate. She had been a Christian for nearly twenty years and possessed godly wisdom. Hana and I became the best of friends.

One evening, Hana and I were approached by two men as we were leaving the vegetable market. They ordered Hana to leave me alone with them. When she refused, they slapped her in the face and knocked the bag of vegetables from her arms. Immediately, she knelt down and began to pray. The two men repeatedly slapped me in the face with the back of their hands, six or seven times each. Suddenly, I could hear police whistles. The two men ran away, but not before they threatened me exclaiming, "Christians are corrupting the world. Give up your job and return home or die."

Hana and I filed a police report, but we knew nothing would be done. When my father heard of the attack, he came to Kiev to see me. He was very upset with the police for not taking the event more seriously. Nonetheless, even with his influence, the event was dismissed as insignificant. Hana and I decided to vary our times and routes to and from the market. I am not sure that we were any safer, but we felt safer.

The two of us continued sharing a flat and teaching at the school until Hana's mother became sick and she went home to care for her. I was so sad to see her go. She had been such an incredible blessing to me, and I learned so much from her. From time to time, I still think of her and how much fun we had together. Some of my fondest memories are of the two of us singing in the church choir. Anytime either of us would hit a note off-key, the other one would just look, smile, and keep on singing.

When Hana left, God provided Sarah, a teacher from America. Sarah moved into the flat with me, and we, too, quickly became friends. Sarah was more intent on sharing her faith with non-Christians than Hana or I. After living with Sarah for a little less than a year, I learned to be bolder. Sarah and I had been witnessing to Leena, a waitress in the café just around the corner from our flat. One evening, as we were leaving the café just after dusk, we turned the corner and two men approached us. Immediately, I was fearful. It seemed I was about to be attacked again.

One of the two men worked in the café and had been listening in on the conversations of Sarah and me for some time. He had also overheard us talking with Leena. I relaxed a little but could tell by the look on his face that something was terribly wrong. He started to say vile things to Sarah and me. He degraded Sarah until I had to speak up.

"Leave her alone. This woman is a gift from God to the Ukrainian people. She has been sent here to tell of the love of God for us. Leave her alone."

As soon as I finished saying this, I felt this warm, wet sensation in my side. I had been stabbed with a knife or some sharp object. It did not hurt, but blood was running down my side and dripping onto the sidewalk.

Sarah gasped, and I watched the man from the café pull a metal blade from her chest, which was at least six inches long and dripping with blood. Sarah collapsed on the sidewalk and I knelt down over her. The two men quickly ran off as I ran into the café and asked the owner to call for an ambulance. It took the ambulance twenty minutes to arrive. When they arrived, I was still holding the bottom of my skirt to Sarah's chest in an effort to stop the blood. Sarah was not conscious, and I was afraid she was dead. I did not realize how serious my injury was. As a matter of fact, I had forgotten about it until the ambulance driver noticed it.

We were taken to the hospital. I was in surgery for a little over an hour, but Sarah was in for eight hours. Her wounds were much worse than mine. I was released the following day, but Sarah remained in the hospital for three weeks. Due to the severity of her injuries, Sarah thought it best to return to America.

After two weeks of home recovery, I went back to teaching. With Sarah going to the United States, life seemed cold and empty. I was alone in my flat and terrified to walk anywhere by myself. Every time I met a man on the street, my heart would stop. I would hold my breath until he passed by. I became more discontent with life. I began to wonder if Jesus even cared for me, I was in such a deep depression. But God took notice of my plight.

In October, my mother visited me. When she arrived, she handed me a present. She said, "Oksana, your father and I are concerned for you. You need help. I have kept this tucked away and hidden for over twenty-five years now. Maybe it will help you. It sure seemed to help Mama [my grandmother]." It was an old Bible from the early 1900s. It was my grandmother's Bible!

Just holding it made me feel better. Somehow it linked me to my grandmother. When I began to read the notes she had made in the margins, I was fascinated. My grandmother had written notes to herself on nearly every aspect of life. I watched God at work in her life which, in turn, brought healing to my own life. And I was reading the notes sixty, seventy, and even eighty years after they were written. I think the words that helped me the most went something like this:

You [Jesus] are my strength, my shield, my fortress, and my reason for living. The communists have been searching house-to-house confiscating Bibles and Christian artifacts. They have harassed my fellow brothers and sisters for too long now. Please intervene on our behalf. The communists have taken Bibles from so many of my close friends. Please do not let them find my Bible. I need it for nourishment. I hunger for You, and desperately desire the day I will finally see You face to face. Oh, dear Jesus, even if they take my Bible they cannot take You away. If they take everything from me, even my life, it is fine with me.

Wait, Jesus, please forgive me. I am being selfish. Let the communists and the whole world, for that matter, do as they will with me. There is only one thing I ask of You. Please let my life honor and glorify You. All I need is You.

I cried all night after reading my grandmother's thoughts. I realized that I was wrong to be bitter at God for allowing me to be attacked. I fell to my knees and begged Jesus for forgiveness. I sensed a cleansed heart that I had not felt in months. I read every one of my grandmother's three hundred and twelve notations, and I, too, decided that all I needed was Jesus. My outlook changed.

I went back to the café and told the man who stabbed Sarah and me, and who never was arrested, that I forgave him. I shared the gospel of Jesus Christ with him and testified to him, "Jesus loves you, even if you do not love Him."

At this time, God has provided me with a new roommate. Timsala is a teacher from India who has a master's degree in primary education and a doctorate in intercultural communications. She will only be here for a year, but we are already becoming the best of friends. Timsala has encouraged me to continue my education and pursue higher degrees. So I may go back to school in a year or so. There is a university in Odessa, near the home my parents recently purchased, and I may just choose to move back to the town in which I grew up. Perhaps I can sit on the rooftop and watch the harbor boats and great ships as they cruise the Black Sea, as I did when I was a little girl.

The view will be the same, but my perspective in life has changed considerably. As a little girl, I was raised to be both educated and a devout atheist. I was brought up adhering to the Communist worldview, a system that is following Dylan Thomas's advice: "Do not go gentle into that good night." In many parts of Ukraine, the older generation would prefer to go back to the oppressive times. "At least we were fed well and taken care of," they say. Some younger Ukrainians are attempting to seek power by reviving the old coalition of Orthodox Church and the state. If my country moves in either of these directions, we evangelicals will pay a heavy price.

My life serves as a good illustration that persecution—whether it comes from religion, atheism, or a totally secular government—still exists. It is a good reminder that Christians, wherever they live, are only one generation from persecution. Persecution is never desirable, and although citizens need to rise up to stand for freedom, Christians must prepare themselves for whatever comes our way.

May it be that if the Lord tarries His coming and the next generation opens their Bibles, we are found faithful to the Lord with our very lives like my grandmother. May the margins of our Bibles show the courage of our hearts.

The Ultimate Sacrifice
The Story of Hassan and Ali
(Saudi Arabia)

*And they cried with a loud voice, saying,
"How long, O Lord, holy and true, until You judge and
avenge our blood on those who dwell on the earth?" And
a white robe was given to each of them; and it was said to
them that they should rest a little while longer, until both
the number of their fellow servants and their brethren, who
would be killed as they were, was completed.*
—REVELATION 6:10–11

I thought that I had experienced all the pain a man could endure. Years ago, my family paid the ultimate price for their conversion to Christianity. My memory is vivid of the senseless, brutal beating of my mother and of seeing her lifeless body lying on the bedroom floor. Later, as my father and I were attempting to escape the wrath of officials of our homeland, I saw him savagely gunned down, shot in the back three times. I can still feel the touch of my father's hand as it slipped from mine. His body sank into the warm waters by the shore on the straits of Malacca. I chronicled this difficult journey in *The Costly Call: Modern-Day Stories of Muslims Who Found Jesus*. But the rough road I traveled was not yet over.

Recently I received news that Ali, a good friend, had been sentenced to death in Saudi Arabia. Ali had turned his back on Islam and embraced the teachings of Jesus—a crime punishable by death according to Muhammad himself (Hadith 9.57). Ali was not openly espousing Christianity or attempting to convert Muslims to Jesus. He was simply trying to live daily life by the teachings of Jesus. The Saudi High Court found him guilty of treason against the Qur'an. Ali was to be beheaded in a few days.

My mind raced to put together a plan to rescue Ali. I could not let my friend be put to death. I believe God has given me a divine call to rescue former Muslims who are being savagely persecuted for their faith in Jesus and are in grave danger. To date, the Lord has allowed me to liberate more than two dozen of His saints.

Even though we only had a little more than a week to prepare for the operation, we swiftly put all the details in place for Ali's rescue. Two men were assigned to pick up Ali's wife and three-year-old daughter while four men and I would rescue Ali as he was transported into the desert. We would rendezvous off the coast of Gibraltar on a small fishing vessel. My contact at the embassy was to meet us there with proper immigration papers for everyone in the family. The family would be given a brand new beginning in life.

We arrived in the country undetected, and everyone was in place. At first, nothing seemed abnormal, but that changed when we arrived at the camp where Ali was supposedly incarcerated. At 3:30 AM, I was watching for movement inside the compound and noticed that the surroundings were unusually quiet. There were only two guards on duty, which raised questions in my mind, since normally there were at least four, if not six. I am not sure exactly what went wrong, but suddenly I felt cold steel pressing against the base of my neck. Then I heard the sound "CLICK!"

No one had to clue me in to that sound. I knew it well from days gone by. It was the sound of a soldier's rifle as he cocked the hammer in preparation to fire. For a moment, I believed he was going to pull the trigger and send me into the presence of Jesus. But instead he spoke to me in Arabic: "Infidel, get up. Come with me."

I had been caught. Without another word, the Saudi soldier escorted me into the compound and placed me in a cell. However, Ali was not in the compound. He had been moved. Someone had sold us out, but who would do such a thing? I did not sleep for the next few hours. I prayed and asked the Lord for wisdom.

The next morning I was interrogated for four hours. Even though I never told the officials who I was or why I was in Saudi Arabia, they had all the details. The fact is, I had been compromised. Later that day, I was transported for two hours to a remote site in the desert where I was placed in a cell next to Ali. We were both shocked to see each other. He had no idea that I was coming as I had been overly careful to communicate my plans only to those who needed to know them.

I think the Saudis put us together in hopes that we would talk and reveal some sinister master plan to rescue Christians from the country. The Saudis consistently exterminate former Muslims who convert to Christianity. Perhaps they also wanted Ali to witness the magistrate sentencing me to death as well. They take pleasure in such sadism.

Later that night, when I shared with Ali my failed plan to rescue him, he wept for me. "Hassan, my dear brother, you have put your life in danger for me. You are too valuable to the Lord's work. You should not be here." Then he prayed for two hours begging Jesus to rescue *me!* With no thought for his own death, Ali begged Jesus to save me from the wrath of the Saudis.

Ali and I reminisced and prayed together all night. Even though I thought that I would be executed the next morning, that was the best night of my life. There I was, just me, an old friend, and Jesus sitting in a jail cell in Saudi Arabia. It seemed eerily like something the apostle Paul would have done. It truly was a blessed moment. I will treasure that day always, for that night I found out that, not only was Ali dear to me, but I was dear to him. Oh, that we all might have an Ali in our lives.

Sunrise came early. Ali and I did not sleep a wink. We simply talked to Jesus and each other. There was no last meal, no big breakfast with fanfare, no cigars or last words, nothing romantic like the movies portray, just a simple walk to death. The jailors unlocked our cells and escorted us before the magistrate. We were forced to kneel before him. He looked at Ali and exclaimed, "Take his head." He turned to me and said, "Take him to Riyadh to be shot."

Ali was dragged face down to the execution area, and his wife and daughter were brought out to witness the execution. It was then that I realized just how bad the situation really was. I had hoped that at least Ali's family had been rescued. All kinds of thoughts went racing through my mind. Had every aspect of the rescue failed? How did the Saudis find out? Who sold me out? God, where are You in this?

Suddenly, a soldier grabbed me by the arm and escorted me to stand by Ali's wife and little three-year-old daughter. I could barely breathe as I looked into their eyes. My heart felt as though it would explode from my chest. How could these self-righteous Saudi Muslims force this precious little girl to watch as her daddy's head was severed from his body? I had to remind myself that they were just following the teachings of Muhammad, the beloved founder of their faith. He was brutal to men, women, and children.

One soldier took a four-foot piece of rope and tied Ali's hands together behind his back. Another soldier grabbed a longer piece of rope and looped it around Ali's neck. He was forced to kneel down over a wooden block, which stood three feet from the ground. One soldier stood behind Ali tightly gripping the rope securing Ali's hands. The other soldier stretched Ali's neck out across the wooden block by placing his foot on the base of the block and pulling the rope around Ali's neck until he was gasping for breath. There was no way Ali could move. His death would be swift and certain.

Ali's wife was weeping uncontrollably. I was holding his precious little daughter trying to shield her eyes with my right hand from what was about to happen. Providentially, Ali's head was slightly turned toward us, and we could see his eyes as the executioner raised the sword. Amazingly, there was no fear in his eyes. As a matter of fact, it seemed Ali was actually looking forward to this moment.

Within an instant the executioner began his downward swing toward Ali's neck, and the soldier holding the rope slightly eased the rope's tension. In that moment of time, I heard Ali say, "Father, into your hands I commit my spirit." Then I watched as my dearest brother, Ali, went to be with his blessed Jesus. With an echoing thud, his head separated from his body and Ali was immediately in the presence of Jesus. The soldiers just let Ali's separated body and head lie in the dust. As I watched Ali's blood cover the ground, I knew that it had been spilled in devotion for his Savior. I pray that when my time comes, I, too, will be so devoted to my Jesus.

Ali's wife, daughter, and I were immediately swept away and loaded into a military vehicle with four soldiers. An hour and a half into the journey to Riyadh, the vehicle stopped to investigate an accident on the road ahead. It appeared that a couple of cars had crashed on the highway. One of the cars was belching smoke as though it were burning up. Just as the four soldiers stepped from the transport, I heard what sounded like a single gunshot. I grabbed Ali's wife and daughter and tried to shield them with my body. Then I saw that all four soldiers were lying on the ground. The gunshot I heard had actually been four simultaneous gunshots.

As I opened the door, four men ran up to me, four of the men I had hired to assist me in my rescue attempt of Ali. They had been watching the situation and waiting for an opportunity to free me.

At first, I was so relieved, but my relief turned to guilt. Around me lay four dead Muslims who would spend eternity separated from the love of Jesus, and now they had no opportunity to hear of His love. I felt as though they had died at my expense. The thought kept running through my mind, "Why Lord? Why Lord? Why didn't you just take me?" Then I remembered Ali's prayer from the night before, "Lord, please rescue my friend, Hassan." God had answered the prayer of a righteous man.

My friends quickly escorted Ali's wife, daughter, and me to the coast and put us on a fishing vessel bound for Gibraltar. All of us prayed during the entire voyage. It was the most solemn time of my life. I had failed in rescuing my friend, and I had cost four Muslims their lives. I am still trying to make sense of it all.

As I reflect on the entire event, I now realize that the Lord is using this time to remind me of one of His truths. Jesus is in absolute control in the affairs of Christians. We will die when He deems that it is our time, and we will not die until He chooses. In essence, no man can extend his life one second beyond that moment that Jesus wishes, nor can any man take a Christian's life until the moment Jesus wishes.

Even though Ali's execution was brutal—especially since it was done in front of his family—it was done in God's timing. I know that I will see Ali one day in heaven. How I look forward to that day when I see Jesus, Mom, Dad, and Ali.

My deepest regret is that four lost men went into a Christless eternity. I am not sure what my future holds, but the Lord has carefully prepared me for it through past tragedies. I have devoted my life to the rescue of former Muslims who have come to faith in Christ and who face severe persecution and death. Out of some twenty-eight or so attempts, this was my first failure. And since Jesus is in control, I guess it was not really a failure. Ali is free and with his Lord. His wife and daughter are here with me, and I will provide for their needs. I also will continue doing exactly what God has called me to do: "Rescue the perishing."

The Voice of the Martyrs

Serving the persecuted church since 1967

The Voice of the Martyrs is a non-profit, interdenominational organization dedicated to assisting the persecuted church worldwide. VOM was founded more than thirty-five years ago by Pastor Richard Wurmbrand, who was imprisoned in communist Romania for fourteen years for his faith in Jesus Christ. His wife, Sabina, was imprisoned for three years. In the 1960s, Richard, Sabina, and their son, Mihai, were ransomed out of Romania and came to the United States. Through their travels the Wurmbrands spread the message of the atrocities that Christians face in restricted nations, while establishing a network of offices dedicated to assisting the persecuted church. The Voice of the Martyrs continues in this mission around the world today through its main purposes:

1. To encourage and empower Christians to fulfill the Great Commission in areas of the world where they are persecuted for their involvement in propagating the gospel of Jesus Christ. We accomplish this by providing Bibles, literature, radio broadcasts, medical assistance, and other forms of aid.
2. To give relief to the families of Christian martyrs in these areas of the world.
3. To equip local Christians to win to Christ those persecutors who are opposed to the gospel in countries where believers are actively persecuted for their Christian witness.
4. To undertake projects of encouragement, helping believers rebuild their lives and Christian witness in countries that have formerly suffered communist oppression.
5. To emphasize the fellowship of all believers by informing the world of atrocities committed against Christians and by remembering their courage and faith.

The Voice of the Martyrs publishes a free, monthly newsletter giving updates on the persecuted church and ways you can help.

To subscribe, call or write:

The Voice of the Martyrs
P.O. Box 54
Caney, KS 67333
(800) 747-0085
E-mail address: thevoice@vom-usa.org
Web site: www.persecution.com

Emir Fethi Caner (Ph.D., University of Texas at Arlington) is currently dean of The College at Southwestern (Southwestern Seminary) as well as professor of history and director of the Center for Free Church Studies. An award-winning and best-selling author, he speaks regularly on apologetics, world religions, and theology around the world and on such media outlets as NPR, PAX, and Billy Graham's *Decision Today* radio program. His past experience includes pastoring, overseas missions, and church planting.

H. Edward Pruitt (M. Div., Southeastern Baptist Theological Seminary), coauthor of *The Costly Call: Modern-Day Stories of Muslims Who Found Christ*, has traveled nearly two million miles and worked extensively with missionaries in more than sixty countries. He is the associate director of the Center for Great Commissions Studies at Southeastern Seminary in Wake Forest. He is currently working toward a doctorate of theology at the University of South Africa. Ed speaks at mission conferences globally, and has been interviewed through numerous media outlets nationwide.

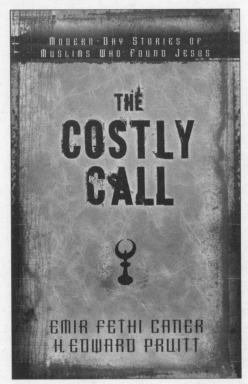

MODERN-DAY STORIES OF
MUSLIMS WHO FOUND JESUS

THE
COSTLY
CALL

EMIR FETHI CANER
H. EDWARD PRUITT

THE COSTLY CALL
Modern-Day Stories of
Muslims Who Found Jesus
0-8254-3555-2 • 160 pages

These are the tales of the untold heroes of the Christian faith, those rejected, tortured, and killed because of the One they chose to follow. Hassan, Aisha, Wan Mae, Adahiem . . . Malaysia, Saudi Arabia, China, Egypt . . . and many others. These are their true stories.

"Vividly and forcefully but empathetically, The Costly Call *paints real-life word pictures of crosses borne by Muslims who truly follow Christ. Read it and weep! Read it and rejoice! Read it and understand!"*
—DAVID J. HESSELGRAVE
Professor Emeritus of Missions
Trinity Evangelical Divinity School